The Science of the Blockchain

Roger Wattenhofer

Copyright © 2016 by Roger Wattenhofer
First Edition 2016
Inverted Forest Publishing
ISBN-13 978-1522751830
ISBN-10 1522751831

Preface

When hanging out with colleagues from financial technology (FinTech), you cannot help but notice that the so-called *blockchain* is all the rage, almost as important as the Internet. Some FinTech colleagues seem to understand the blockchain as a magic piece of code that allows the participants of a distributed system to agree on a common view of the system, to track changes in the system. In the distributed systems community, agreement techniques have been known long before cryptocurrencies such as Bitcoin (where the term blockchain is borrowed) emerged. Various concepts and protocols exist, each with its own advantages and disadvantages.

The idea of this book is to give a scientifically precise overview of the most interesting approaches that have emerged in the past few decades. If you are a developer (in FinTech or not), this book will help you to get a better understanding what is right and what is wrong for your distributed system, what is possible and what is not.

This Book

This book introduces the basic techniques when building fault-tolerant distributed systems. We will present different protocols and algorithms that allow for fault-tolerant operation, and we will discuss practical systems that implement these techniques.

The book presents the main ideas independently from each other, each topic has its own chapter. Each chapter starts with an introductory story that motivates the content of the chapter. Algorithms, protocols and definitions are presented formally, so that you know how to implement the ideas. Some insights are proved in theorems, so that you learn why the concepts or algorithms are correct, and what they can guarantee. Most of the other text is presented as so-called remarks. These remarks discuss various informal thoughts, and often set the stage for the next idea. However, one will get the essence of each chapter even without reading any of these remarks. Each chapter also discusses the history of the ideas presented in the chapter, so that you can find the original research.

In this book, we will see different models (and combinations of models) that may make sense in different scenarios. The focus of the book is on protocols and systems that matter in practice. In other words, we do not discuss concepts because they are fun, but because they are practically relevant.

Nevertheless, have fun!

Contents

1 Introduction   1
    1.1 What are Distributed Systems? 1
    1.2 Book Overview 2

2 Fault-Tolerance & Paxos   5
    2.1 Client/Server 5
    2.2 Paxos 10

3 Consensus   17
    3.1 Two Friends 17
    3.2 Consensus 18
    3.3 Impossibility of Consensus 18
    3.4 Randomized Consensus 25
    3.5 Shared Coin 29

4 Byzantine Agreement   33
    4.1 Validity 34
    4.2 How Many Byzantine Nodes? 35
    4.3 The King Algorithm 38
    4.4 Lower Bound on Number of Rounds 40
    4.5 Asynchronous Byzantine Agreement 40

5 Authenticated Agreement   45
    5.1 Agreement with Authentication 45
    5.2 Zyzzyva 47

6 Quorum Systems   61
    6.1 Load and Work 62
    6.2 Grid Quorum Systems 64
    6.3 Fault Tolerance 66
    6.4 Byzantine Quorum Systems 70

7 Eventual Consistency & Bitcoin   77
   7.1 Consistency, Availability and Partitions   78
   7.2 Bitcoin   79
   7.3 Smart Contracts   87
   7.4 Weak Consistency   91

8 Distributed Storage   95
   8.1 Consistent Hashing   95
   8.2 Hypercubic Networks   97
   8.3 DHT & Churn 105

Chapter 1

Introduction

1.1 What are Distributed Systems?

Today's computing and information systems are inherently *distributed*. Many companies are operating on a global scale, with thousands or even millions of machines on all the continents. Data is stored in various data centers, computing tasks are performed on multiple machines.

At the other end of the spectrum, also your mobile phone is a distributed system. Not only does it probably share some of your data with the cloud, also the phone itself contains multiple processing and storage units.

Moreover, computers have come a long way. In the early 1970s, microchips featured a clock rate of roughly 1 MHz. 10 years later, in the early 1980s, you could get a computer with a clock rate of roughly 10 MHz. In the early 1990s, clock speed was around 100 Mhz. In the early 2000s the first 1 GHz processor was shipped to customers. Just a few years later, in the Mid 2000s, one could already buy processors with clock rates between 3 and 4 GHz. If you buy a new computer today, chances are that the clock rate is still between 3 and 4 GHz, since clock rates basically stopped growing after about 2004. Clock speed can apparently not be increased without running into physical issues such as overheating.

In summary, today almost all computer systems are distributed, for different reasons:

- Geography: Large organizations and companies are inherently geographically distributed.

- Parallelism: In order to speed up computation, we employ multicore processors or computing clusters.

- Reliability: Data is replicated on different machines in order to prevent loss.

- Availability: Data is replicated on different machines in order to allow for fast access, without bottleneck, minimizing latency.

Even though distributed systems have many benefits, such as increased storage, computational power, or even the possibility to connect spatially separated locations, they also introduce challenging *coordination* problems. Coordination problems are so prevalent, they come with various flavors and names: Blockchain, consistency, agreement, consensus, ledger, event sourcing, etc.

Coordination problems will happen quite often in a distributed system. Even though every single node (computer, core, network switch, etc.) of a distributed system will only fail once every few years, with millions of nodes, you can expect a failure every minute. On the bright side, one may hope that a distributed system with multiple nodes may tolerate some failures and continue to work correctly.

1.2 Book Overview

The central concept of this book will be introduced in Chapter 2 and is generally known as *state replication*, see Definition 2.8. We achieve state replication if all nodes of a distributed system agree on a sequence of commands, the same set of commands in the same order. In the financial tech industry, state replication is often synonymous with the term blockchain. State replication can be achieved using various algorithms, depending on the failures the system must be able to tolerate.

In Chapter 2 we will motivate and introduce the basic definitions, and present Paxos, an algorithm that achieves state replication even though a minority of nodes in the system may crash.

In Chapter 3 we will understand that Paxos may not make progress, and that indeed no deterministic protocol can solve state replication if we are unlucky. However, on the positive side, we will also introduce a fast randomized consensus protocol that can solve state replication despite crash failures.

In Chapter 4 we look beyond simple crash failures, and introduce protocols that work even in the presence of malicious behavior, in synchronous and asynchronous systems. In addition, we will explore different definitions for correct behavior.

In Chapter 5 we use a cryptographic concept called message authentication. We first present a simple synchronous protocol, and then Zyzzyva, a state of the art asynchronous protocol for implementing state replication if message authentication is available.

In Chapter 6 we investigate scalability issues by studying so-called quorum systems. If a set of servers is no longer powerful enough, and adding more servers does not help, quorum systems may be an elegant solution.

In Chapter 7 we introduce weaker consistency concepts, and provide a detailed explanation of the Bitcoin protocol as a prime example of such a protocol.

Finally, in Chapter 8 we explore even weaker consistency concepts, and present highly scalable distributed storage solutions.

Chapter Notes

Many good text books have been written on the subject, e.g. [AW04, CGR11, CDKB11, Lyn96, Mul93, Ray13, TS01]. James Aspnes has written an excellent freely available script on distributed systems [Asp14]. Similarly to our course, these texts focus on large-scale distributed systems, and hence there is some overlap with our course. There are also some excellent text books focusing on small-scale multicore systems, e.g. [HS08].

Some colleagues have helped writing and improving this book. Thanks go to Pascal Bissig, Philipp Brandes, Christian Decker, Klaus-Tycho Förster, Barbara Keller, Rik Melis, and David Stolz, in alphabetical order.

Bibliography

[Asp14] James Aspnes. Notes on Theory of Distributed Systems, 2014.

[AW04] Hagit Attiya and Jennifer Welch. *Distributed Computing: Fundamentals, Simulations and Advanced Topics (2nd edition)*. John Wiley Interscience, March 2004.

[CDKB11] George Coulouris, Jean Dollimore, Tim Kindberg, and Gordon Blair. *Distributed Systems: Concepts and Design*. Addison-Wesley Publishing Company, USA, 5th edition, 2011.

[CGR11] Christian Cachin, Rachid Guerraoui, and Lus Rodrigues. *Introduction to Reliable and Secure Distributed Programming*. Springer Publishing Company, Incorporated, 2nd edition, 2011.

[HS08] Maurice Herlihy and Nir Shavit. *The Art of Multiprocessor Programming*. Morgan Kaufmann Publishers Inc., San Francisco, CA, USA, 2008.

[Lyn96] Nancy A. Lynch. *Distributed Algorithms*. Morgan Kaufmann Publishers Inc., San Francisco, CA, USA, 1996.

[Mul93] Sape Mullender, editor. *Distributed Systems (2Nd Ed.)*. ACM Press/Addison-Wesley Publishing Co., New York, NY, USA, 1993.

[Ray13] Michel Raynal. *Distributed Algorithms for Message-Passing Systems*. Springer Publishing Company, Incorporated, 2013.

[TS01] Andrew S. Tanenbaum and Maarten Van Steen. *Distributed Systems: Principles and Paradigms*. Prentice Hall PTR, Upper Saddle River, NJ, USA, 1st edition, 2001.

Chapter 2

Fault-Tolerance & Paxos

How do you create a fault-tolerant distributed system? In this chapter we start out with simple questions, and, step by step, improve our solutions until we arrive at a system that works even under adverse circumstances, Paxos.

2.1 Client/Server

Definition 2.1 (node)**.** *We call a single actor in the system* **node***. In a computer network the computers are the nodes, in the classical client-server model both the server and the client are nodes, and so on. If not stated otherwise, the total number of nodes in the system is n.*

Model 2.2 (message passing)**.** *In the* **message passing model** *we study distributed systems that consist of a set of nodes. Each node can perform local computations, and can send messages to every other node.*

Remarks:

- We start with two nodes, the smallest number of nodes in a distributed system. We have a *client* node that wants to "manipulate" data (e.g., store, update, ...) on a remote *server* node.

Algorithm 2.3 Naïve Client-Server Algorithm

1: Client sends commands one at a time to server

Model 2.4 (message loss). *In the message passing model with **message loss**, for **any** specific message, it is not guaranteed that it will arrive safely at the receiver.*

Remarks:

- A related problem is message corruption, i.e., a message is received but the content of the message is corrupted. In practice, in contrast to message loss, message corruption can be handled quite well, e.g. by including additional information in the message, such as a checksum.

- Algorithm 2.3 does not work correctly if there is message loss, so we need a little improvement.

Algorithm 2.5 Client-Server Algorithm with Acknowledgments

1: Client sends commands one at a time to server
2: Server acknowledges every command
3: If the client does not receive an acknowledgment within a reasonable time, the client resends the command
---

Remarks:

- Sending commands "one at a time" means that when the client sent command c, the client does not send any new command c' until it received an acknowledgment for c.

- Since not only messages sent by the client can be lost, but also acknowledgments, the client might resend a message that was already received and executed on the server. To prevent multiple executions of the same command, one can add a *sequence number* to each message, allowing the receiver to identify duplicates.

- This simple algorithm is the basis of many reliable protocols, e.g. TCP.

- The algorithm can easily be extended to work with multiple servers: The client sends each command to every

2.1. CLIENT/SERVER

server, and once the client received an acknowledgment from each server, the command is considered to be executed successfully.

- What about multiple clients?

Model 2.6 (variable message delay). *In practice, messages might experience different transmission times, even if they are being sent between the same two nodes.*

Remarks:

- Throughout this chapter, we assume the variable message delay model.

Theorem 2.7. *If Algorithm 2.5 is used with multiple clients and multiple servers, the servers might see the commands in different order, leading to an inconsistent state.*

Proof. Assume we have two clients u_1 and u_2, and two servers s_1 and s_2. Both clients issue a command to update a variable x on the servers, initially $x = 0$. Client u_1 sends command $x = x + 1$ and client u_2 sends $x = 2 \cdot x$.

Let both clients send their message at the same time. With variable message delay, it can happen that s_1 receives the message from u_1 first, and s_2 receives the message from u_2 first.[1] Hence, s_1 computes $x = (0 + 1) \cdot 2 = 2$ and s_2 computes $x = (0 \cdot 2) + 1 = 1$. □

Definition 2.8 (state replication). *A set of nodes achieves **state replication**, if all nodes execute a (potentially infinite) sequence of commands $c_1, c_2, c_3, \ldots$, in the same order.*

Remarks:

- State replication is a fundamental property for distributed systems.

- For people working in the financial tech industry, state replication is often synonymous with the term blockchain. The Bitcoin blockchain we will discuss in Chapter 7 is indeed one way to implement state replication. However, as we will see in all the other chapters, there are many alternative concepts that are worth knowing, with different properties.

---

[1] For example, u_1 and s_1 are (geographically) located close to each other, and so are u_2 and s_2.

- Since state replication is trivial with a single server, we can designate a single server as a *serializer*. By letting the serializer distribute the commands, we automatically order the requests and achieve state replication!

Algorithm 2.9 State Replication with a Serializer
1: Clients send commands one at a time to the serializer
2: Serializer forwards commands one at a time to all other servers
3: Once the serializer received all acknowledgments, it notifies the client about the success

---

Remarks:

- This idea is sometimes also referred to as *master-slave replication*.

- What about node failures? Our serializer is a single point of failure!

- Can we have a more *distributed* approach of solving state replication? Instead of directly establishing a consistent order of commands, we can use a different approach: We make sure that there is always at most one client sending a command; i.e., we use *mutual exclusion*, respectively *locking*.

Algorithm 2.10 Two-Phase Protocol

Phase 1

1: Client asks all servers for the lock

Phase 2

2: **if** client receives lock from every server **then**
3:     Client sends command reliably to each server, and gives the lock back
4: **else**
5:     Clients gives the received locks back
6:     Client waits, and then starts with Phase 1 again
7: **end if**

2.1. CLIENT/SERVER

Remarks:

- This idea appears in many contexts and with different names, usually with slight variations, e.g. *two-phase locking (2PL)*.

- Another example is the *two-phase commit (2PC)* protocol, typically presented in a database environment. The first phase is called the *preparation* of a transaction, and in the second phase the transaction is either *committed* or *aborted*. The 2PC process is not started at the client but at a designated server node that is called the *coordinator*.

- It is often claimed that 2PL and 2PC provide better consistency guarantees than a simple serializer if nodes can *recover* after crashing. In particular, alive nodes might be kept consistent with crashed nodes, for transactions that started while the crashed node was still running. This benefit was even improved in a protocol that uses an additional phase (3PC).

- The problem with 2PC or 3PC is that they are not well-defined if exceptions happen.

- Does Algorithm 2.10 really handle node crashes well? No! In fact, it is even worse than the simple serializer approach (Algorithm 2.9): Instead of having a only one node which must be available, Algorithm 2.10 requires *all* servers to be responsive!

- Does Algorithm 2.10 also work if we only get the lock from a subset of servers? Is a majority of servers enough?

- What if two or more clients concurrently try to acquire a majority of locks? Do clients have to abandon their already acquired locks, in order not to run into a deadlock? How? And what if they crash before they can release the locks? Do we need a slightly different concept?

2.2 Paxos

Definition 2.11 (ticket). *A **ticket** is a weaker form of a lock, with the following properties:*

- **Reissuable:** *A server can issue a ticket, even if previously issued tickets have not yet been returned.*

- **Ticket expiration:** *If a client sends a message to a server using a previously acquired ticket t, the server will only accept t, if t is the most recently issued ticket.*

Remarks:

- There is no problem with crashes: If a client crashes while holding a ticket, the remaining clients are not affected, as servers can simply issue new tickets.

- Tickets can be implemented with a counter: Each time a ticket is requested, the counter is increased. When a client tries to use a ticket, the server can determine if the ticket is expired.

- What can we do with tickets? Can we simply replace the locks in Algorithm 2.10 with tickets? We need to add at least one additional phase, as only the client knows if a majority of the tickets have been valid in Phase 2.

2.2. PAXOS

Algorithm 2.12 Naïve Ticket Protocol

Phase 1

1: Client asks all servers for a ticket

Phase 2

2: **if** a majority of the servers replied **then**
3:    Client sends command together with ticket to each server
4:    Server stores command only if ticket is still valid, and replies to client
5: **else**
6:    Client waits, and then starts with Phase 1 again
7: **end if**

Phase 3

8: **if** client hears a positive answer from a majority of the servers **then**
9:    Client tells servers to execute the stored command
10: **else**
11:    Client waits, and then starts with Phase 1 again
12: **end if**

Remarks:

- There are problems with this algorithm: Let u_1 be the first client that successfully stores its command c_1 on a majority of the servers. Assume that u_1 becomes very slow just before it can notify the servers (Line 7), and a client u_2 updates the stored command in some servers to c_2. Afterwards, u_1 tells the servers to execute the command. Now some servers will execute c_1 and others c_2!

- How can this problem be fixed? We know that every client u_2 that updates the stored command after u_1 must have used a newer ticket than u_1. As u_1's ticket was accepted in Phase 2, it follows that u_2 must have acquired its ticket after u_1 already stored its value in the respective server.

- Idea: What if a server, instead of only handing out tickets in Phase 1, also notifies clients about its currently stored command? Then, u_2 learns that u_1 already stored c_1 and instead of trying to store c_2, u_2 could support u_1 by also storing c_1. As both clients try to store and execute the same command, the order in which they proceed is no longer a problem.

- But what if not all servers have the same command stored, and u_2 learns multiple stored commands in Phase 1. What command should u_2 support?

- Observe that it is always safe to support the most recently stored command. As long as there is no majority, clients can support any command. However, once there is a majority, clients need to support this value.

- So, in order to determine which command was stored most recently, servers can remember the ticket number that was used to store the command, and afterwards tell this number to clients in Phase 1.

- If every server uses its own ticket numbers, the newest ticket does not necessarily have the largest number. This problem can be solved if clients suggest the ticket numbers themselves!

2.2. PAXOS

Algorithm 2.13 Paxos

Client (Proposer)	Server (Acceptor)

Initialization ....

c ◁ *command to execute* $T_{\max} = 0$ ◁ *largest issued ticket*
$t = 0$ ◁ *ticket number to try*

$C = \bot$ ◁ *stored command*
$T_{\text{store}} = 0$ ◁ *ticket used to store C*

Phase 1 ....

1: $t = t + 1$
2: Ask all servers for ticket t

3: **if** $t > T_{\max}$ **then**
4:     $T_{\max} = t$
5:     Answer with $\text{ok}(T_{\text{store}}, C)$
6: **end if**

Phase 2 ....

7: **if** a majority answers ok **then**
8:     Pick (T_{store}, C) with largest T_{store}
9:     **if** $T_{\text{store}} > 0$ **then**
10:         $c = C$
11:     **end if**
12:     Send $\text{propose}(t, c)$ to same majority
13: **end if**

14: **if** $t = T_{\max}$ **then**
15:     $C = c$
16:     $T_{\text{store}} = t$
17:     Answer success
18: **end if**

Phase 3 ....

19: **if** a majority answers success **then**
20:     Send $\text{execute}(c)$ to every server
21: **end if**

Remarks:

- Unlike previously mentioned algorithms, there is no step where a client explicitly decides to start a new attempt and jumps back to Phase 1. Note that this is not necessary, as a client can decide to abort the current attempt and start a new one *at any point* in the algorithm. This has the advantage that we do not need to be careful about selecting "good" values for timeouts, as correctness is independent of the decisions when to start new attempts.

- The performance can be improved by letting the servers send negative replies in phases 1 and 2 if the ticket expired.

- The contention between different clients can be alleviated by randomizing the waiting times between consecutive attempts.

Lemma 2.14. *We call a message* propose(t,c) *sent by clients on Line 12 a **proposal for (t,c)**. A proposal for (t,c) is **chosen**, if it is stored by a majority of servers (Line 15). For every issued* propose(t',c') *with $t' > t$ holds that $c' = c$, if there was a chosen* propose(t,c).

Proof. Observe that there can be at most one proposal for every ticket number τ since clients only send a proposal if they received a majority of the tickets for τ (Line 7). Hence, every proposal is uniquely identified by its ticket number τ.

Assume that there is at least one propose(t',c') with $t' > t$ and $c' \neq c$; of such proposals, consider the proposal with the smallest ticket number t'. Since both this proposal and also the propose(t,c) have been sent to a majority of the servers, we can denote by S the non-empty intersection of servers that have been involved in both proposals. Recall that since propose(t,c) has been chosen, this means that that at least one server $s \in S$ must have stored command c; thus, when the command was stored, the ticket number t was still valid. Hence, s must have received the request for ticket t' *after* it already stored propose(t,c), as the request for ticket t' invalidates ticket t.

Therefore, the client that sent propose(t',c') must have learned from s that a client already stored propose(t,c). Since a client adapts its proposal to the command that is stored with the highest ticket number so far (Line 8), the client must have proposed c as well. There is only one possibility that would lead to the client not adapting c: If the client received the information from a server that some client stored propose(t^*,c^*), with $c^* \neq c$ and $t^* > t$. But in that case, a client must have sent propose(t^*,c^*) with $t < t^* < t'$, but this contradicts the assumption that t' is the smallest ticket number of a proposal issued after t. □

Theorem 2.15. *If a command c is executed by some servers, all servers (eventually) execute c.*

Proof. From Lemma 2.14 we know that once a proposal for c is chosen, every subsequent proposal is for c. As there is exactly one first propose(t,c) that is chosen, it follows that all successful proposals will be for the command c. Thus, only proposals for a single command c can be chosen, and since clients only tell servers

2.2. PAXOS

to execute a command, when it is chosen (Line 20), each client will eventually tell every server to execute c. □

Remarks:

- If the client with the first successful proposal does not crash, it will directly tell every server to execute c.

- However, if the client crashes before notifying any of the servers, the servers will execute the command only once the next client is successful. Once a server received a request to execute c, it can inform every client that arrives later that there is already a chosen command, so that the client does not waste time with the proposal process.

- Note that Paxos cannot make progress if half (or more) of the servers crash, as clients cannot achieve a majority anymore.

- The original description of Paxos uses three roles: Proposers, acceptors and learners. Learners have a trivial role: They do nothing, they just learn from other nodes which command was chosen.

- We assigned every node only one role. In some scenarios, it might be useful to allow a node to have multiple roles. For example in a peer-to-peer scenario nodes need to act as both client and server.

- Clients (Proposers) must be trusted to follow the protocol strictly. However, this is in many scenarios not a reasonable assumption. In such scenarios, the role of the proposer can be executed by a set of servers, and clients need to contact proposers, to propose values in their name.

- So far, we only discussed how a set of nodes can reach decision for a single command with the help of Paxos. We call such a single decision an *instance* of Paxos.

- If we want to execute multiple commands, we can extend each instance with an instance number, that is sent around with every message. Once a command is chosen, any client can decide to start a new instance with the next number. If a server did not realize that the previous instance came to a decision, the server can ask other servers about the decisions to catch up.

Chapter Notes

Two-phase protocols have been around for a long time, and it is unclear if there is a single source of this idea. One of the earlier descriptions of this concept can found in the book of Gray [Gra78].

Leslie Lamport introduced Paxos in 1989. But why is it called Paxos? Lamport described the algorithm as the solution to a problem of the parliament of a fictitious Greek society on the island Paxos. He even liked this idea so much, that he gave some lectures in the persona of an Indiana-Jones-style archaeologist! When the paper was submitted, many readers were so distracted by the descriptions of the activities of the legislators, they did not understand the meaning and purpose of the algorithm. The paper was rejected. But Lamport refused to rewrite the paper, and he later wrote that he *"was quite annoyed at how humorless everyone working in the field seemed to be"*. A few years later, when the need for a protocol like Paxos arose again, Lamport simply took the paper out of the drawer and gave it to his colleagues. They liked it. So Lamport decided to submit the paper (in basically unaltered form!) again, 8 years after he wrote it – and it got accepted! But as this paper [Lam98] is admittedly hard to read, he had mercy, and later wrote a simpler description of Paxos [Lam01].

Bibliography

[Gra78] James N. Gray. *Notes on data base operating systems.* Springer, 1978.

[Lam98] Leslie Lamport. The part-time parliament. *ACM Transactions on Computer Systems (TOCS)*, 16(2):133–169, 1998.

[Lam01] Leslie Lamport. Paxos made simple. *ACM Sigact News*, 32(4):18–25, 2001.

Chapter 3

Consensus

3.1 Two Friends

Alice wants to arrange dinner with Bob, and since both of them are very reluctant to use the "call" functionality of their phones, she sends a text message suggesting to meet for dinner at 6pm. However, texting is unreliable, and Alice cannot be sure that the message arrives at Bob's phone, hence she will only go to the meeting point if she receives a confirmation message from Bob. But Bob cannot be sure that his confirmation message is received; if the confirmation is lost, Alice cannot determine if Bob did not even receive her suggestion, or if Bob's confirmation was lost. Therefore, Bob demands a confirmation message from Alice, to be sure that she will be there. But as this message can also be lost...

You can see that such a message exchange continues forever, if both Alice and Bob want to be sure that the other person will come to the meeting point!

Remarks:

- Such a protocol cannot terminate: Assume that there are protocols which lead to agreement, and P is one of the protocols which require the least number of messages. As the last confirmation might be lost and the protocol still needs to guarantee agreement, we can simply decide to always omit the last message. This gives us a new protocol P' which requires less messages than P, contradicting the assumption that P required the minimal amount of messages.

- Can Alice and Bob use Paxos?

3.2 Consensus

In Chapter 2 we studied a problem that we vaguely called agreement. We will now introduce a formally specified variant of this problem, called *consensus*.

Definition 3.1 (consensus). *There are n nodes, of which at most f might crash, i.e., at least $n - f$ nodes are **correct**. Node i starts with an input value v_i. The nodes must decide for one of those values, satisfying the following properties:*

- **Agreement** *All correct nodes decide for the same value.*
- **Termination** *All correct nodes terminate in finite time.*
- **Validity** *The decision value must be the input value of a node.*

Remarks:

- We assume that every node can send messages to every other node, and that we have reliable links, i.e., a message that is sent will be received.
- There is no broadcast medium. If a node wants to send a message to multiple nodes, it needs to send multiple individual messages.
- Does Paxos satisfy all three criteria? If you study Paxos carefully, you will notice that Paxos does not guarantee termination. For example, the system can be stuck forever if two clients continuously request tickets, and neither of them ever manages to acquire a majority.

3.3 Impossibility of Consensus

Model 3.2 (asynchronous). *In the **asynchronous model**, algorithms are event based ("upon receiving message ..., do ...''). Nodes do not have access to a synchronized wall-clock. A message sent from one node to another will arrive in a finite but unbounded time.*

3.3. IMPOSSIBILITY OF CONSENSUS

Remarks:

- The asynchronous time model is a widely used formalization of the variable message delay model (Model 2.6).

Definition 3.3 (asynchronous runtime). *For algorithms in the asynchronous model, the **runtime** is the number of time units from the start of the execution to its completion in the worst case (every legal input, every execution scenario), assuming that each message has a delay of **at most** one time unit.*

Remarks:

- The maximum delay cannot be used in the algorithm design, i.e., the algorithm must work independent of the actual delay.

- Asynchronous algorithms can be thought of as systems, where local computation is significantly faster than message delays, and thus can be done in no time. Nodes are only active once an event occurs (a message arrives), and then they perform their actions "immediately".

- We will show now that crash failures in the asynchronous model can be quite harsh. In particular there is no deterministic fault-tolerant consensus algorithm in the asynchronous model, not even for binary input.

Definition 3.4 (configuration). *We say that a system is fully defined (at any point during the execution) by its **configuration** C. The configuration includes the state of every node, and all messages that are in transit (sent but not yet received).*

Definition 3.5 (univalent). *We call a configuration C **univalent**, if the decision value is determined independently of what happens afterwards.*

Remarks:

- We call a configuration that is univalent for value v v-valent.

- Note that a configuration can be univalent, even though no single node is aware of this. For example, the configuration in which all nodes start with value 0 is 0-valent (due to the validity requirement).

- As we restricted the input values to be binary, the decision value of any consensus algorithm will also be binary (due to the validity requirement).

Definition 3.6 (bivalent). *A configuration C is called **bivalent** if the nodes might decide for 0 or 1.*

Remarks:

- The decision value depends on the order in which messages are received or on crash events. I.e., the decision is not yet made.

- We call the initial configuration of an algorithm C_0. When nodes are in C_0, all of them executed their initialization code and possibly sent some messages, and are now waiting for the first message to arrive.

Lemma 3.7. *There is at least one selection of input values V such that the according initial configuration C_0 is bivalent, if $f \geq 1$.*

Proof. Note that C_0 only depends on the input values of the nodes, as no event occurred yet. Let $V = [v_0, v_1, \ldots, v_{n-1}]$ denote the array of input values, where v_i is the input value of node i.

We construct $n+1$ arrays $V_0, V_1, \ldots, V_n$, where the index i in V_i denotes the position in the array up to which all input values are 1. So, $V_0 = [0, 0, 0, \ldots, 0]$, $V_1 = [1, 0, 0, \ldots, 0]$, and so on, up to $V_n = [1, 1, 1, \ldots, 1]$.

Note that the configuration corresponding to V_0 must be 0-valent so that the validity requirement is satisfied. Analogously, the configuration corresponding to V_n must be 1-valent. Assume that all initial configurations with starting values V_i are univalent. Therefore, there must be at least one index b, such that the configuration corresponding to V_b is 0-valent, and configuration corresponding to V_{b+1} is 1-valent. Observe that only the input value of the bth node differs from V_b to V_{b+1}.

Since we assumed that the algorithm can tolerate at least one failure, i.e., $f \geq 1$, we look at the following execution: All nodes except b start with their initial value according to V_b respectively V_{b+1}. Node b is "extremely slow"; i.e., all messages sent by b are scheduled in such a way, that all other nodes must assume that b crashed, in order to satisfy the termination requirement. Since the nodes cannot determine the value of b, and we assumed that all initial configurations are univalent, they will decide for a value v

3.3. IMPOSSIBILITY OF CONSENSUS

independent of the initial value of b. Since V_b is 0-valent, v must be 0. However we know that V_{b+1} is 1-valent, thus v must be 1. Since v cannot be both 0 and 1, we have a contradiction.

□

Definition 3.8 (transition). *A **transition** from configuration C to a following configuration C_τ is characterized by an event $\tau = (u, m)$, i.e., node u receiving message m.*

Remarks:

- Transitions are the formally defined version of the "events" in the asynchronous model we described before.
- A transition $\tau = (u, m)$ is only applicable to C, if m was still in transit in C.
- C_τ differs from C as follows: m is no longer in transit, u has possibly a different state (as u can update its state based on m), and there are (potentially) new messages in transit, sent by u.

Definition 3.9 (configuration tree). *The **configuration tree** is a directed tree of configurations. Its root is the configuration C_0 which is fully characterized by the input values V. The edges of the tree are the transitions; every configuration has all applicable transitions as outgoing edges.*

Remarks:

- For any algorithm, there is exactly *one* configuration tree for every selection of input values.
- Leaves are configurations where the execution of the algorithm terminated. Note that we use termination in the sense that the system as a whole terminated, i.e., there will not be any transition anymore.
- Every path from the root to a leaf is one possible asynchronous execution of the algorithm.
- Leaves must be univalent, or the algorithm terminates without agreement.
- If a node u crashes when the system is in C, all transitions $(u, *)$ are removed from C in the configuration tree.

Lemma 3.10. *Assume two transitions $\tau_1 = (u_1, m_1)$ and $\tau_2 = (u_2, m_2)$ for $u_1 \neq u_2$ are both applicable to C. Let $C_{\tau_1 \tau_2}$ be the configuration that follows C by first applying transition τ_1 and then τ_2, and let $C_{\tau_2 \tau_1}$ be defined analogously. It holds that $C_{\tau_1 \tau_2} = C_{\tau_2 \tau_1}$.*

Proof. Observe that τ_2 is applicable to C_{τ_1}, since m_2 is still in transit and τ_1 cannot change the state of u_2. With the same argument τ_1 is applicable to C_{τ_2}, and therefore both $C_{\tau_1 \tau_2}$ and $C_{\tau_2 \tau_1}$ are well-defined. Since the two transitions are completely independent of each other, meaning that they consume the same messages, lead to the same state transitions and to the same messages being sent, it follows that $C_{\tau_1 \tau_2} = C_{\tau_2 \tau_1}$. □

Definition 3.11 (critical configuration). *We say that a configuration C is **critical**, if C is bivalent, but all configurations that are direct children of C in the configuration tree are univalent.*

Remarks:

- Informally, C is critical, if it is the last moment in the execution where the decision is not yet clear. As soon as the next message is processed by any node, the decision will be determined.

Lemma 3.12. *If a system is in a bivalent configuration, it must reach a critical configuration within finite time, or it does not always solve consensus.*

Proof. Recall that there is at least one bivalent initial configuration (Lemma 3.7). Assuming that this configuration is not critical, there must be at least one bivalent following configuration; hence, the system may enter this configuration. But if this configuration is not critical as well, the system may afterwards progress into another bivalent configuration. As long as there is no critical configuration, an unfortunate scheduling (selection of transitions) can always lead the system into another bivalent configuration. The only way how an algorithm can *enforce* to arrive in a univalent configuration is by reaching a critical configuration.

Therefore we can conclude that a system which does not reach a critical configuration has at least one possible execution where it will terminate in a bivalent configuration (hence it terminates without agreement), or it will not terminate at all. □

3.3. IMPOSSIBILITY OF CONSENSUS

Lemma 3.13. *If a configuration tree contains a critical configuration, crashing a single node can create a bivalent leaf; i.e., a crash prevents the algorithm from reaching agreement.*

Proof. Let C denote critical configuration in a configuration tree, and let T be the set of transitions applicable to C. Let $\tau_0 = (u_0, m_0) \in T$ and $\tau_1 = (u_1, m_1) \in T$ be two transitions, and let C_{τ_0} be 0-valent and C_{τ_1} be 1-valent. Note that T must contain these transitions, as C is a critical configuration.

Assume that $u_0 \neq u_1$. Using Lemma 3.10 we know that C has a following configuration $C_{\tau_0 \tau_1} = C_{\tau_1 \tau_0}$. Since this configuration follows C_{τ_0} it must be 0-valent. However, this configuration also follows C_{τ_1} and must hence be 1-valent. This is a contradiction and therefore $u_0 = u_1$ must hold.

Therefore we can pick one particular node u for which there is a transition $\tau = (u, m) \in T$ which leads to a 0-valent configuration. As shown before, all transitions in T which lead to a 1-valent configuration must also take place on u. Since C is critical, there must be at least one such transition. Applying the same argument again, it follows that all transitions in T that lead to a 0-valent configuration must take place on u as well, and since C is critical, there is no transition in T that leads to a bivalent configuration. Therefore *all* transitions applicable to C take place on the *same* node u!

If this node u crashes while the system is in C, *all transitions are removed*, and therefore the system is stuck in C, i.e., it terminates in C. But as C is critical, and therefore bivalent, the algorithm fails to reach an agreement. $\square$

Theorem 3.14. *There is no deterministic algorithm which always achieves consensus in the asynchronous model, with $f > 0$.*

Proof. We assume that the input values are binary, as this is the easiest non-trivial possibility. From Lemma 3.7 we know that there must be at least one bivalent initial configuration C. Using Lemma 3.12 we know that if an algorithm solves consensus, all executions starting from the bivalent configuration C must reach a critical configuration. But if the algorithm reaches a critical configuration, a single crash can prevent agreement (Lemma 3.13). $\square$

Remarks:

- If $f = 0$, then each node can simply send its value to all others, wait for all values, and choose the minimum.

- But if a single node may crash, there is no deterministic solution to consensus in the asynchronous model.

- How can the situation be improved? For example by giving each node access to randomness, i.e., we allow each node to toss a coin.

3.4 Randomized Consensus

Algorithm 3.15 Randomized Consensus (Ben-Or)
1: $v_i \in \{0, 1\}$ ◁ input bit
2: round = 1
3: decided = false

4: Broadcast myValue(v_i, round)

5: **while** true **do**

   Propose

6:   Wait until a majority of myValue messages of current round arrived
7:   **if** all messages contain the same value v **then**
8:      Broadcast propose(v, round)
9:   **else**
10:     Broadcast propose($\bot$, round)
11: **end if**

12: **if** decided **then**
13:     Broadcast myValue(v_i, round+1)
14:     Decide for v_i and terminate
15: **end if**

   Adapt

16: Wait until a majority of propose messages of current round arrived
17: **if** all messages propose the same value v **then**
18:     $v_i = v$
19:     decide = true
20: **else if** there is at least one proposal for v **then**
21:     $v_i = v$
22: **else**
23:     Choose v_i randomly, with $Pr[v_i = 0] = Pr[v_i = 1] = 1/2$
24: **end if**
25: round = round + 1
26: Broadcast myValue(v_i, round)
27: **end while**

Remarks:

- The idea of Algorithm 3.15 is very simple: Either all nodes start with the same input bit, which makes consensus easy. Otherwise, nodes toss a coin until a large number of nodes get – by chance – the same outcome.

Lemma 3.16. *As long as no node sets **decided** to true, Algorithm 3.15 always makes progress, independent of which nodes crash.*

Proof. The only two steps in the algorithm when a node waits are in Lines 6 and 15. Since a node only waits for a majority of the nodes to send a message, and since $f < n/2$, the node will always receive enough messages to continue, as long as no correct node set its value decided to true and terminates. □

Lemma 3.17. *Algorithm 3.15 satisfies the validity requirement.*

Proof. Observe that the validity requirement of consensus, when restricted to binary input values, corresponds to: If all nodes start with v, then v must be chosen; otherwise, either 0 or 1 is acceptable, and the validity requirement is automatically satisfied.

Assume that all nodes start with v. In this case, all nodes propose v in the first round. As all nodes only hear proposals for v, all nodes decide for v (Line 17) and exit the loop in the following round. □

Lemma 3.18. *Algorithm 3.15 satisfies the agreement requirement.*

Proof. Observe that proposals for both 0 and 1 cannot occur in the same round, as nodes only send a proposal for v, if they hear a *majority* for v in Line 8.

Let u be the first node that decides for a value v in round r. Hence, it received a majority of proposals for v in r (Line 17). Note that once a node receives a majority of proposals for a value, it will adapt this value and terminate in the next round. Since there cannot be a proposal for any other value in r, it follows that no node decides for a different value in r.

In Lemma 3.16 we only showed that nodes make progress as long as no node decides, thus we need to be careful that no node gets stuck if u terminates.

Any node $u' \neq u$ can experience one of two scenarios: Either it also receives a majority for v in round r and decides, or it does not receive a majority. In the first case, the agreement requirement

3.4. RANDOMIZED CONSENSUS

is directly satisfied, and also the node cannot get stuck. Let us study the latter case. Since u heard a majority of proposals for v, it follows that every node hears *at least one* proposal for v. Hence, all nodes set their value v_i to v in round r. Therefore, all nodes will broadcast v at the end of round r, and thus all nodes will propose v in round $r + 1$. The nodes that already decided in round r will terminate in $r+1$ and send one additional myValue message (Line 13). All other nodes will receive a majority of proposals for v in $r + 1$, and will set decided to true in round $r + 1$, and also send a myValue message in round $r + 1$. Thus, in round $r + 2$ some nodes have already terminated, and others hear enough myValue messages to make progress in Line 6. They send another propose and a myValue message and terminate in $r + 2$, deciding for the same value v. □

Lemma 3.19. *Algorithm 3.15 satisfies the termination requirement, i.e., all nodes terminate in expected time $O(2^n)$.*

Proof. We know from the proof of Lemma 3.18 that once a node hears a majority of proposals for a value, all nodes will terminate at most two rounds later. Hence, we only need to show that a node receives a majority of proposals for the same value within expected time $O(2^n)$.

Assume that no node receives a majority of proposals for the same value. In such a round, some nodes may update their value to v based on a proposal (Line 20). As shown before, all nodes that update the value based on a proposal, adapt the same value v. The rest of the nodes choses 0 or 1 randomly. The probability that all nodes choose the same value v in one round is hence at least $1/2^n$. Therefore, the expected number of rounds is bounded by $O(2^n)$. As every round consists of two message exchanges, the asymptotic runtime of the algorithm is equal to the number of rounds. □

Theorem 3.20. *Algorithm 3.15 achieves binary consensus with expected runtime $O(2^n)$ if up to $f < n/2$ nodes crash.*

Remarks:

- How good is a fault tolerance of $f < n/2$?

Theorem 3.21. *There is no consensus algorithm for the asynchronous model that tolerates $f \geq n/2$ many failures.*

Proof. Assume that there is an algorithm that can handle $f = n/2$ many failures. We partition the set of all nodes into two sets N, N' both containing $n/2$ many nodes. Let us look at three different selection of input values: In V_0 all nodes start with 0. In V_1 all nodes start with 1. In V_{half} all nodes in N start with 0, and all nodes in N' start with 1.

Assume that nodes start with V_{half}. Since the algorithm must solve consensus independent of the scheduling of the messages, we study the scenario where all messages sent from nodes in N to nodes in N' (or vice versa) are heavily delayed. Note that the nodes in N cannot determine if they started with V_0 or V_{half}. Analogously, the nodes in N' cannot determine if they started in V_1 or V_{half}. Hence, if the algorithm terminates before any message from the other set is received, N must decide for 0 and N' must decide for 1 (to satisfy the validity requirement, as they could have started with V_0 respectively V_1). Therefore, the algorithm would fail to reach agreement.

The only possibility to overcome this problem is to wait for at least one message sent from a node of the other set. However, as $f = n/2$ many nodes can crash, the entire other set could have crashed before they sent any message. In that case, the algorithm would wait forever and therefore not satisfy the termination requirement. □

Remarks:

- Algorithm 3.15 solves consensus with optimal fault-tolerance – but it is awfully slow. The problem is rooted in the individual coin tossing: If all nodes toss the same coin, they could terminate in a constant number of rounds.

- Can this problem be fixed by simply always choosing 1 at Line 22?!

- This cannot work: Such a change makes the algorithm deterministic, and therefore it cannot achieve consensus (Theorem 3.14). Simulating what happens by always choosing 1, one can see that it might happen that there is a majority for 0, but a minority with value 1 prevents the nodes from reaching agreement.

- Nevertheless, the algorithm can be improved by tossing a so-called *shared coin*. A shared coin is a random variable

3.5. SHARED COIN

that is 0 for all nodes with constant probability, and 1 with constant probability. Of course, such a coin is not a magic device, but it is simply an algorithm. To improve the expected runtime of Algorithm 3.15, we replace Line 22 with a function call to the shared coin algorithm.

3.5 Shared Coin

Algorithm 3.22 Shared Coin (code for node u)

1: Choose local coin $c_u = 0$ with probability $1/n$, else $c_u = 1$
2: Broadcast myCoin(c_u)

3: Wait for $n - f$ coins and store them in the local coin set C_u
4: Broadcast mySet(C_u)

5: Wait for $n - f$ coin sets
6: **if** at least one coin is 0 among all coins in the coin sets **then**
7:    return 0
8: **else**
9:    return 1
10: **end if**

Remarks:

- Since at most f nodes crash, all nodes will always receive $n - f$ coins respectively coin sets in Lines 3 and 5. Therefore, all nodes make progress and termination is guaranteed.

- We show the correctness of the algorithm for $f < n/3$. To simplify the proof we assume that $n = 3f + 1$, i.e., we assume the worst case.

Lemma 3.23. *Let u be a node, and let W be the set of coins that u received in at least $f + 1$ different coin sets. It holds that $|W| \geq f + 1$.*

Proof. Let C be the multiset of coins received by u. Observe that u receives exactly $|C| = (n - f)^2$ many coins, as u waits for $n - f$ coin sets each containing $n - f$ coins.

Assume that the lemma does not hold. Then, at most f coins are in all $n - f$ coin sets, and all other coins $(n - f)$ are in at most

f coin sets. In other words, the number of total of coins that u received is bounded by

$$|C| \leq f \cdot (n-f) + (n-f) \cdot f = 2f(n-f).$$

Our assumption was that $n > 3f$, i.e., $n - f > 2f$. Therefore $|C| \leq 2f(n-f) < (n-f)^2 = |C|$, which is a contradiction. □

Lemma 3.24. *All coins in W are seen by all correct nodes.*

Proof. Let $w \in W$ be such a coin. By definition of W we know that w is in at least $f+1$ sets received by u. Since every other node also waits for $n - f$ sets before terminating, each node will receive at least one of these sets, and hence w must be seen by every node that terminates. □

Theorem 3.25. *If $f < n/3$ nodes crash, Algorithm 3.22 implements a shared coin.*

Proof. Let us first bound the probability that the algorithm returns 1 for all nodes. With probability $(1-1/n)^n \approx 1/e \approx 0.37$ all nodes chose their local coin equal to 1 (Line 1), and in that case 1 will be decided. This is only a lower bound on the probability that all nodes return 1, as there are also other scenarios based on message scheduling and crashes which lead to a global decision for 1. But a probability of 0.37 is good enough, so we do not need to consider these scenarios.

With probability $1 - (1 - 1/n)^{|W|}$ there is at least one 0 in W. Using Lemma 3.23 we know that $|W| \geq f + 1 \approx n/3$, hence the probability is about $1 - (1 - 1/n)^{n/3} \approx 1 - (1/e)^{1/3} \approx 0.28$. We know that this 0 is seen by all nodes (Lemma 3.24), and hence everybody will decide 0. Thus Algorithm 3.22 implements a shared coin. □

Remarks:

- We only proved the worst case. By choosing f fairly small, it is clear that $f+1 \not\approx n/3$. However, Lemma 3.23 can be proved for $|W| \geq n - 2f$. To prove this claim you need to substitute the expressions in the contradictory statement: At most $n-2f-1$ coins can be in all $n-f$ coin sets, and $n-(n-2f-1) = 2f+1$ coins can be in at most f coin sets. The remainder of the proof is analogous, the only difference is that the math is not as neat. Using the modified Lemma we know that $|W| \geq n/3$, and therefore Theorem 3.25 also holds for *any* $f < n/3$.

- We implicitly assumed that message scheduling was random; if we need a 0 but the nodes that want to propose 0 are "slow", nobody is going to see these 0's, and we do not have progress.

Theorem 3.26. *Plugging Algorithm 3.22 into Algorithm 3.15 we get a randomized consensus algorithm which terminates in a constant expected number of rounds tolerating up to $f < n/3$ crash failures.*

Chapter Notes

The problem of two friends arranging a meeting was presented and studied under many different names; nowadays, it is usually referred to as the *Two Generals Problem*. The impossibility proof was established in 1975 by Akkoyunlu et al. [AEH75].

The proof that there is no deterministic algorithm that always solves consensus is based on the proof of Fischer, Lynch and Paterson [FLP85], known as FLP, which they established in 1985. This result was awarded the 2001 PODC Influential Paper Award (now called Dijkstra Prize). The idea for the randomized consensus algorithm was originally presented by Ben-Or [Ben83]. The concept of a shared coin was introduced by Bracha [Bra87].

Bibliography

[AEH75] EA Akkoyunlu, K Ekanadham, and RV Huber. Some constraints and tradeoffs in the design of network communications. In *ACM SIGOPS Operating Systems Review*, volume 9, pages 67–74. ACM, 1975.

[Ben83] Michael Ben-Or. Another advantage of free choice (extended abstract): Completely asynchronous agreement protocols. In *Proceedings of the second annual ACM symposium on Principles of distributed computing*, pages 27–30. ACM, 1983.

[Bra87] Gabriel Bracha. Asynchronous byzantine agreement protocols. *Information and Computation*, 75(2):130–143, 1987.

[FLP85] Michael J. Fischer, Nancy A. Lynch, and Mike Paterson. Impossibility of Distributed Consensus with One Faulty Process. *J. ACM*, 32(2):374–382, 1985.

Chapter 4
Byzantine Agreement

In order to make flying safer, researchers studied possible failures of various sensors and machines used in airplanes. While trying to model the failures, they were confronted with the following problem: Failing machines did not just crash, instead they sometimes showed arbitrary behavior before stopping completely. With these insights researchers modeled failures as arbitrary failures, not restricted to any patterns.

Definition 4.1 (Byzantine). *A node which can have arbitrary behavior is called **byzantine**. This includes "anything imaginable", e.g., not sending any messages at all, or sending different and wrong messages to different neighbors, or lying about the input value.*

Remarks:

- Byzantine behavior also includes collusion, i.e., all byzantine nodes are being controlled by the same adversary.

- We assume that any two nodes communicate directly, and that no node can forge an incorrect sender address. This is a requirement, such that a single byzantine node cannot simply impersonate all nodes!

- We call non-byzantine nodes *correct* nodes.

Definition 4.2 (Byzantine Agreement). *Finding consensus as in Definition 3.1 in a system with byzantine nodes is called **byzantine agreement**. An algorithm is f-resilient if it still works correctly with f byzantine nodes.*

Remarks:

- As for consensus (Definition 3.1) we also need agreement, termination and validity. Agreement and termination are straight-forward, but what about validity?

4.1 Validity

Definition 4.3 (Any-Input Validity). *The decision value must be the input value of any node.*

Remarks:

- This is the validity definition we implicitly used for consensus, in Definition 3.1.

- Does this definition still make sense in the presence of byzantine nodes? What if byzantine nodes lie about their inputs?

- We would wish for a validity definition which differentiates between byzantine and correct inputs.

Definition 4.4 (Correct-Input Validity). *The decision value must be the input value of a **correct** node.*

Remarks:

- Unfortunately, implementing correct-input validity does not seem to be easy, as a byzantine node following the protocol but lying about its input value is indistinguishable from a correct node. Here is an alternative.

Definition 4.5 (All-Same Validity). *If all correct nodes start with the same input v, the decision value must be v.*

Remarks:

- If the decision values are binary, then correct-input validity is induced by all-same validity.

- If the input values are not binary, but for example from sensors that deliever values in $\mathbb{R}$, all-same validity is in most scenarios not really useful.

Definition 4.6 (Median Validity). *If the input values are orderable, e.g. $v \in \mathbb{R}$, byzantine outliers can be prevented by agreeing on a value close to the median of the correct input values, where close is a function of the number of byzantine nodes f.*

Remarks:

- Is byzantine agreement possible? If yes, with what validity condition?
- Let us try to find an algorithm which tolerates 1 single byzantine node, first restricting to the so-called synchronous model.

Model 4.7 (synchronous). *In the **synchronous model**, nodes operate in synchronous rounds. In each round, each node may send a message to the other nodes, receive the messages sent by the other nodes, and do some local computation.*

Definition 4.8 (synchronous runtime). *For algorithms in the synchronous model, the **runtime** is simply the number of rounds from the start of the execution to its completion in the worst case (every legal input, every execution scenario).*

4.2 How Many Byzantine Nodes?

Algorithm 4.9 Byzantine Agreement with $f = 1$.

1: Code for node u, with input value x:

Round 1

2: Send $\texttt{tuple}(u, x)$ to all other nodes
3: Receive $\texttt{tuple}(v, y)$ from all other nodes v
4: Store all received $\texttt{tuple}(v, y)$ in a set S_u

Round 2

5: Send set S_u to all other nodes
6: Receive sets S_v from all nodes v
7: T = set of $\texttt{tuple}(v, y)$ seen in at least two sets S_v, including own S_u
8: Let $\texttt{tuple}(v, y) \in T$ be the tuple with the smallest value y
9: Decide on value y

Remarks:

- Byzantine nodes may not follow the protocol and send syntactically incorrect messages. Such messages can easily be deteced and discarded. It is worse if byzantine nodes send syntactically correct messages, but with a bogus content, e.g., they send different messages to different nodes.

- Some of these mistakes cannot easily be detected: For example, if a byzantine node sends different values to different nodes in the first round; such values will be put into S_u. However, some mistakes can and must be detected: Observe that all nodes only relay information in Round 2, and do not say anything about their own value. So, if a byzantine node sends a set S_v which contains a `tuple`(v, y), this tuple must be removed by u from S_v upon receiving it (Line 6).

- Recall that we assumed that nodes cannot forge their source address; thus, if a node receives `tuple`(v, y) in Round 1, it is guaranteed that this message was sent by v.

Lemma 4.10. *If $n \geq 4$, all correct nodes have the same set T.*

Proof. With $f = 1$ and $n \geq 4$ we have at least 3 correct nodes. A correct node will see every correct value at least twice, once directly from another correct node, and once through the third correct node. So all correct values are in T. If the byzantine node sends the same value to at least 2 other (correct) nodes, all correct nodes will see the value twice, so all add it to set T. If the byzantine node sends all different values to the correct nodes, none of these values will end up in any set T. □

Theorem 4.11. *Algorithm 4.9 reaches byzantine agreement if $n \geq 4$.*

Proof. We need to show agreement, any-input validity and termination. With Lemma 4.10 we know that all correct nodes have the same set T, and therefore agree on the same minimum value. The nodes agree on a value proposed by any node, so any-input validity holds. Moreover, the algorithm terminates after two rounds. □

4.2. HOW MANY BYZANTINE NODES?

Remarks:

- If $n > 4$ the byzantine node can put multiple values into T.

- The idea of this algorithm can be generalized for any f and $n > 3f$. In the generalization, every node sends in every of $f + 1$ rounds all information it learned so far to all other nodes. In other words, message size increases exponentially with f.

- Does Algorithm 4.9 also work with $n = 3$?

Theorem 4.12. *Three nodes cannot reach byzantine agreement with all-same validity if one node among them is byzantine.*

Proof. We have three nodes u, v, w. In order to achieve all-same validity, a correct node must decide on its own value if another node supports that value. The third node might disagree, but that node could be byzantine. If correct node u has input 0 and correct node v has input 1, the byzantine node w can fool them by telling u that its value is 0 and simultaneously telling v that its value is 1. This leads to u and v deciding on their own values, which results in violating the agreement condition. Even if u talks to v, and they figure out that they have different assumptions about w's value, u cannot distinguish whether w or v is byzantine. □

Theorem 4.13. *A network with n nodes cannot reach byzantine agreement with $f \geq n/3$ byzantine nodes.*

Proof. Let us assume (for the sake of contradiction) that there exists an algorithm A that reaches byzantine agreement for n nodes with $f \geq n/3$ byzantine nodes. With A, we can solve byzantine agreement with 3 nodes. For simplicity, we call the 3 nodes u, v, w supernodes.

Each supernode simulates $n/3$ nodes, either $\lfloor n/3 \rfloor$ or $\lceil n/3 \rceil$, if n is not divisible by 3. Each simulated node starts with the input of its supernode. Now the three supernodes simulate algorithm A. The single byzantine supernode simulates $\lceil n/3 \rceil$ byzantine nodes. As algorithm A promises to solve byzantine agreement for $f \geq n/3$, A has to be able to handle $\lceil n/3 \rceil$ byzantine nodes. Algorithm A guarantees that the correct nodes simulated by the correct two supernodes will achieve byzantine agreement. So the two correct supernodes can just take the value of their simulated nodes (these values have to be the same by the agreement property), and we have achieved agreement for three supernodes, one of them byzantine. This contradicts Lemma 4.12, hence algorithm A cannot exist. □

4.3 The King Algorithm

Algorithm 4.14 King Algorithm (for $f < n/3$)
1: $x =$ my input value
2: **for** phase $= 1$ to $f + 1$ **do**

   Round 1

3:    Broadcast value(x)

   Round 2

4:    **if** some value(y) at least $n - f$ times **then**
5:        Broadcast propose(y)
6:    **end if**
7:    **if** some propose(z) received more than f times **then**
8:        $x = z$
9:    **end if**

   Round 3

10:   Let node v_i be the predefined king of this phase i
11:   The king v_i broadcasts its current value w
12:   **if** received strictly less than $n - f$ propose(x) **then**
13:       $x = w$
14:   **end if**
15: **end for**

Lemma 4.15. *Algorithm 4.14 fulfills the all-same validity.*

Proof. If all correct nodes start with the same value, all correct nodes propose it in Round 2. All correct nodes will receive at least $n - f$ proposals, i.e., all correct nodes will stick with this value, and never change it to the king's value. This holds for all phases. □

Lemma 4.16. *If a correct node proposes x, no other correct node proposes y, with $y \neq x$, if $n > 3f$.*

Proof. Assume (for the sake of contradiction) that a correct node proposes value x and another correct node proposes value y. Since a good node only proposes a value if it heard at least $n - f$ value

4.3. THE KING ALGORITHM

messages, we know that both nodes must have received their value from at least $n - 2f$ distinct correct nodes (as at most f nodes can behave byzantine and send x to one node and y to the other one). Hence, there must be a total of at least $2(n - 2f) + f = 2n - 3f$ nodes in the system. Using $3f < n$, we have $2n - 3f > n$ nodes, a contradiction. □

Lemma 4.17. *There is at least one phase with a correct king.*

Proof. There are $f + 1$ phases, each with a different king. As there are only f byzantine nodes, one king must be correct. □

Lemma 4.18. *After a round with a correct king, the correct nodes will not change their values v anymore, if $n > 3f$.*

Proof. If all correct nodes change their values to the king's value, all correct nodes have the same value. If some correct node does not change its value to the king's value, it received a proposal at least $n - f$ times, therefore at least $n - 2f$ correct nodes broadcasted this proposal. Thus, all correct nodes received it at least $n - 2f > f$ times (using $n > 3f$), therefore all correct nodes set their value to the proposed value, including the correct king. Note that only one value can be proposed more than f times, which follows from Lemma 4.16. With Lemma 4.15, no node will change its value after this round. □

Theorem 4.19. *Algorithm 4.14 solves byzantine agreement.*

Proof. The king algorithm reaches agreement as either all correct nodes start with the same value, or they agree on the same value latest after the phase where a correct node was king according to Lemmas 4.17 and 4.18. Because of Lemma 4.15 we know that they will stick with this value. Termination is guaranteed after $3(f + 1)$ rounds, and all-same validity is proved in Lemma 4.15. □

Remarks:

- Algorithm 4.14 requires $f + 1$ predefined kings. We assume that the kings (and their order) are given. Finding the kings indeed would be a byzantine agreement task by itself, so this must be done before the execution of the King algorithm.

- Do algorithms exist which do not need predefined kings? Yes, see Section 4.5.

- Can we solve byzantine agreement (or at least consensus) in less than $f+1$ rounds?

4.4 Lower Bound on Number of Rounds

Theorem 4.20. *A synchronous algorithm solving consensus in the presence of f crashing nodes needs at least $f+1$ rounds, if nodes decide for the minimum seen value.*

Proof. Let us assume (for the sake of contradiction) that some algorithm A solves consensus in f rounds. Some node u_1 has the smallest input value x, but in the first round u_1 can send its information (including information about its value x) to only some other node u_2 before u_1 crashes. Unfortunately, in the second round, the only witness u_2 of x also sends x to exactly one other node u_3 before u_2 crashes. This will be repeated, so in round f only node u_{f+1} knows about the smallest value x. As the algorithm terminates in round f, node u_{f+1} will decide on value x, all other surviving (correct) nodes will decide on values larger than x. □

Remarks:

- A general proof without the restriction to decide for the minimum value exists as well.
- Since byzantine nodes can also just crash, this lower bound also holds for byzantine agreement, so Algorithm 4.14 has an asymptotically optimal runtime.
- So far all our byzantine agreement algorithms assume the synchronous model. Can byzantine agreement be solved in the asynchronous model?

4.5 Asynchronous Byzantine Agreement

Lemma 4.22. *Assume $n > 9f$. If a correct node chooses value x in Line 10, then no other correct node chooses value $y \neq x$ in Line 10.*

Proof. For the sake of contradiction, assume that both 0 and 1 are chosen in Line 10. This means that both 0 and 1 had been proposed by at least $n - 5f$ correct nodes. In other words, we have a total of at least $2(n-5f) + f = n + (n-9f) > n$ nodes. Contradiction! □

4.5. ASYNCHRONOUS BYZANTINE AGREEMENT

Algorithm 4.21 Asynchronous Byzantine Agreement (Ben-Or, for $f < n/9$)

1: $x_i \in \{0, 1\}$ ◁ input bit
2: r = 1 ◁ round
3: decided = false
4: Broadcast propose(x_i,r)
5: **repeat**
6:    Wait until $n-f$ propose messages of current round r arrived
7:    **if** at least $n - 2f$ propose messages contain the same value x **then**
8:       $x_i = x$, decided = true
9:    **else if** at least $n - 4f$ propose messages contain the same value x **then**
10:       $x_i = x$
11:    **else**
12:       choose x_i randomly, with $Pr[x_i = 0] = Pr[x_i = 1] = 1/2$
13:    **end if**
14:    r = r + 1
15:    Broadcast propose(x_i,r)
16: **until** decided (see Line 8)
17: decision = x_i

Theorem 4.23. *Algorithm 4.21 solves binary byzantine agreement as in Definition 4.2 for up to $f < n/9$ byzantine nodes.*

Proof. First note that it is not a problem to wait for $n - f$ propose messages in Line 6, since at most f nodes are byzantine. If all correct nodes have the same input value x, then all (except the f byzantine nodes) will propose the same value x. Thus, every node receives at least $n - 2f$ propose messages containing x, deciding on x in the first round already. We have established all-same validity! If the correct nodes have different (binary) input values, the validity condition becomes trivial as any result is fine.

What about agreement? Let u be the first node to decide on value x (in Line 8). Due to asynchrony another node v received messages from a different subset of the nodes, however, at most f senders may be different. Taking into account that byzantine nodes may lie (send different propose messages to different nodes), f additional propose messages received by v may differ from those received by u. Since node u had at least $n - 2f$ propose messages with value x, node v has at least $n-4f$ propose messages with value

x. Hence every correct node will propose x in the next round, and then decide on x.

So we only need to worry about termination: We have already seen that as soon as one correct node terminates (Line 8) everybody terminates in the next round. So what are the chances that some node u terminates in Line 8? Well, we can hope that all correct nodes randomly propose the same value (in Line 12). Maybe there are some nodes not choosing at random (entering Line 10 instead of 12), but according to Lemma 4.22 they will all propose the same.

Thus, at worst all $n - f$ correct nodes need to randomly choose the same bit, which happens with probability $2^{-(n-f)+1}$. If so, all correct nodes will send the same propose message, and the algorithm terminates. So the expected running time is exponential in the number of nodes n. □

Remarks:

- This Algorithm is a proof of concept that asynchronous byzantine agreement can be achieved. Unfortunately this algorithm is not useful in practice, because of its runtime.

- For a long time, there was no algorithm with subexponential runtime. The currently fastest algorithm has an expected runtime of $O(n^{2.5})$ but only tolerates $f \leq 1/500n$ many byzantine nodes. This algorithm works along the lines of the shared coin algorithm; additionally nodes try to detect which nodes are byzantine.

Chapter Notes

The project which started the study of byzantine failures was called SIFT and was founded by NASA [WLG+78], and the research regarding byzantine agreement started to get significant attention with the results by Pease, Shostak, and Lamport [PSL80, LSP82]. In [PSL80] they presented the generalized version of Algorithm 4.9 and also showed that byzantine agreement is unsolvable for $n \leq 3f$. The algorithm presented in that paper is nowadays called *Exponential Information Gathering (EIG)*, due to the exponential size of the messages.

There are many algorithms for the byzantine agreement problem. For example the Queen Algorithm [BG89] which has a better runtime than the King algorithm [BGP89], but tolerates less failures. That byzantine agreement requires at least $f+1$ many rounds was shown by Dolev and Strong [DS83], based on a more complicated proof from Fischer and Lynch [FL82].

While many algorithms for the synchronous model have been around for a long time, the asynchronous model is a lot harder. The only results were by Ben-Or and Bracha. Ben-Or [Ben83] was able to tolerate $f < n/5$. Bracha [BT85] improved this tolerance to $f < n/3$. The first algorithm with a polynomial expected runtime was found by King and Saia [KS13] just recently.

Nearly all developed algorithms only satisfy all-same validity. There are a few exceptions, e.g., correct-input validity [FG03], available if the initial values are from a finite domain, or median validity [SW15] if the input values are orderable.

Before the term *byzantine* was coined, the terms Albanian Generals or Chinese Generals were used in order to describe malicious behavior. When the involved researchers met people from these countries they moved – for obvious reasons – to the historic term byzantine [LSP82].

Bibliography

[Ben83] Michael Ben-Or. Another advantage of free choice (extended abstract): Completely asynchronous agreement protocols. In *Proceedings of the second annual ACM symposium on Principles of distributed computing*, pages 27–30. ACM, 1983.

[BG89] Piotr Berman and Juan A Garay. *Asymptotically optimal distributed consensus*. Springer, 1989.

[BGP89] Piotr Berman, Juan A. Garay, and Kenneth J. Perry. Towards optimal distributed consensus (extended abstract). In *30th Annual Symposium on Foundations of Computer Science, Research Triangle Park, North Carolina, USA, 30 October - 1 November 1989*, pages 410–415, 1989.

[BT85] Gabriel Bracha and Sam Toueg. Asynchronous consensus and broadcast protocols. *Journal of the ACM (JACM)*, 32(4):824–840, 1985.

[DS83] Danny Dolev and H. Raymond Strong. Authenticated

algorithms for byzantine agreement. *SIAM Journal on Computing*, 12(4):656–666, 1983.

[FG03] Matthias Fitzi and Juan A Garay. Efficient player-optimal protocols for strong and differential consensus. In *Proceedings of the twenty-second annual symposium on Principles of distributed computing*, pages 211–220. ACM, 2003.

[FL82] Michael J. Fischer and Nancy A. Lynch. A lower bound for the time to assure interactive consistency. 14(4):183–186, June 1982.

[KS13] Valerie King and Jared Saia. Byzantine agreement in polynomial expected time:[extended abstract]. In *Proceedings of the forty-fifth annual ACM symposium on Theory of computing*, pages 401–410. ACM, 2013.

[LSP82] Leslie Lamport, Robert E. Shostak, and Marshall C. Pease. The byzantine generals problem. *ACM Trans. Program. Lang. Syst.*, 4(3):382–401, 1982.

[PSL80] Marshall C. Pease, Robert E. Shostak, and Leslie Lamport. Reaching agreement in the presence of faults. *J. ACM*, 27(2):228–234, 1980.

[SW15] David Stolz and Roger Wattenhofer. Byzantine Agreement with Median Validity. In *19th International Conference on Priniciples of Distributed Systems (OPODIS), Rennes, France*, 2015.

[WLG+78] John H. Wensley, Leslie Lamport, Jack Goldberg, Milton W. Green, Karl N. Levitt, P. M. Melliar-Smith, Robert E. Shostak, and Charles B. Weinstock. Sift: Design and analysis of a fault-tolerant computer for aircraft control. In *Proceedings of the IEEE*, pages 1240–1255, 1978.

Chapter 5

Authenticated Agreement

Byzantine nodes are able to lie about their inputs as well as received messages. Can we detect certain lies and limit the power of byzantine nodes? Possibly, the authenticity of messages may be validated using signatures?

5.1 Agreement with Authentication

Definition 5.1 (Signature). *If a node never signs a message, then no correct node ever accepts that message. We denote a message $\texttt{msg}(x)$ signed by node u with $\texttt{msg}(x)_u$.*

Remarks:

- Algorithm 5.2 shows an agreement protocol for binary inputs relying on signatures. We assume there is a designated "primary" node p. The goal is to decide on p's value.

Algorithm 5.2 Byzantine Agreement with Authentication

Code for primary p:

1: **if** input is 1 **then**
2:     broadcast $\text{value}(1)_p$
3:     decide 1 and terminate
4: **else**
5:     decide 0 and terminate
6: **end if**

Code for all other nodes v:

7: **for all** rounds $i \in 1, \ldots, f+1$ **do**
8:     S is the set of accepted messages $\text{value}(1)_u$.
9:     **if** $|S| \geq i$ and $\text{value}(1)_p \in S$ **then**
10:        broadcast $S \cup \{\text{value}(1)_v\}$
11:        decide 1 and terminate
12:    **end if**
13: **end for**
14: decide 0 and terminate

Theorem 5.3. *Algorithm 5.2 can tolerate $f < n$ byzantine failures while terminating in $f + 1$ rounds.*

Proof. Assuming that the primary p is not byzantine and its input is 1, then p broadcasts $\text{value}(1)_p$ in the first round, which will trigger all correct nodes to decide for 1. If p's input is 0, there is no signed message $\text{value}(1)_p$, and no node can decide for 1.

If primary p is byzantine, we need all correct nodes to decide for the same value for the algorithm to be correct. Let us assume that p convinces a correct node v that its value is 1 in round i with $i < f + 1$. We know that v received i signed messages for value 1. Then, v will broadcast $i + 1$ signed messages for value 1, which will trigger all correct nodes to also decide for 1. If p tries to convince some node v late (in round $i = f + 1$), v must receive $f + 1$ signed messages. Since at most f nodes are byzantine, at least one correct node u signed a message $\texttt{value}(1)_u$ in some round $i < f+1$, which puts us back to the previous case. □

Remarks:

- The algorithm only takes $f+1$ rounds, which is optimal as described in Theorem 4.20.

- Using signatures, Algorithm 5.2 solves consensus for any number of failures! Does this contradict Theorem 4.12? Recall that in the proof of Theorem 4.12 we assumed that a byzantine node can distribute contradictory information about its own input. If messages are signed, correct nodes can detect such behavior – a node u signing two contradicting messages proves to all nodes that node u is byzantine.

- Does Algorithm 5.2 satisfy any of the validity conditions introduced in Section 4.1? No! A byzantine primary can dictate the decision value. Can we modify the algorithm such that the correct-input validity condition is satisfied? Yes! We can run the algorithm in parallel for $2f+1$ primary nodes. Either 0 or 1 will occur at least $f+1$ times, which means that one correct process had to have this value in the first place. In this case, we can only handle $f < \frac{n}{2}$ byzantine nodes.

- In reality, a primary will usually be correct. If so, Algorithm 5.2 only needs two rounds! Can we make it work with arbitrary inputs? Also, relying on synchrony limits the practicality of the protocol. What if messages can be lost or the system is asynchronous?

- Zyzzyva uses authenticated messages to achieve state replication, as in Definition 2.8. It is designed to run fast when nodes run correctly, and it will slow down to fix failures!

5.2 Zyzzyva

Definition 5.4 (View). *A view V describes the current state of a replicated system, enumerating the $3f+1$ replicas. The view V also marks one of the replicas as the primary p.*

Definition 5.5 (Command). *If a client wants to update (or read) data, it sends a suitable command c in a* Request *message to the primary p. Apart from the command c itself, the* Request *message also includes a timestamp t. The client signs the message to guarantee authenticity.*

Definition 5.6 (History). *The history h is a sequence of commands $c_1, c_2, \ldots$ in the order they are executed by Zyzzyva. We denote the history up to c_k with h_k.*

Remarks:

- In Zyzzyva, the primary p is used to order commands submitted by clients to create a history h.
- Apart from the globally accepted history, node u may also have a local history, which we denote as h^u or h_k^u.

Definition 5.7 (Complete command). *If a command completes, it will remain in its place in the history h even in the presence of failures.*

Remarks:

- As long as clients wait for the completion of their commands, clients can treat Zyzzyva like one single computer even if there are up to f failures.

In the Absence of Failures

Algorithm 5.8 Zyzzyva: No failures

1: At time t client u wants to execute command c
2: Client u sends request $\mathtt{R} = \mathtt{Request}(c,t)_u$ to primary p
3: Primary p appends c to its local history, i.e., $h^p = (h^p, c)$
4: Primary p sends $\mathtt{OR} = \mathtt{OrderedRequest}(h^p, c, \mathtt{R})_p$ to all replicas
5: Each replica r appends command c to local history $h^r = (h^r, c)$ and checks whether $h^r = h^p$
6: Each replica r runs command c_k and obtains result a
7: Each replica r sends $\mathtt{Response}(a,\mathtt{OR})_r$ to client u
8: Client u collects the set S of received $\mathtt{Response}(a,\mathtt{OR})_r$ messages
9: Client u checks if all histories h^r are consistent
10: **if** $|S| = 3f + 1$ **then**
11:     Client u considers command c to be complete
12: **end if**

5.2. ZYZZYVA

Remarks:

- Since the client receives $3f+1$ consistent responses, all correct replicas have to be in the same state.

- Only three communication rounds are required for the command c to complete.

- Note that replicas have no idea which commands are considered complete by clients! How can we make sure that commands that are considered complete by a client are actually executed? We will see in Theorem 5.23.

- Commands received from clients should be ordered according to timestamps to preserve the causal order of commands.

- There is a lot of optimization potential. For example, including the entire command history in most messages introduces prohibitively large overhead. Rather, old parts of the history that are agreed upon can be truncated. Also, sending a hash value of the remainder of the history is enough to check its consistency across replicas.

- What if a client does not receive $3f+1$ $\texttt{Response}(a,\texttt{OR})_r$ messages? A byzantine replica may omit sending anything at all! In practice, clients set a timeout for the collection of Response messages. Does this mean that Zyzzyva only works in the synchronous model? Yes and no. We will discuss this in Lemma 5.26 and Lemma 5.27.

Byzantine Replicas

Algorithm 5.9 Zyzzyva: Byzantine Replicas (append to Algorithm 5.8)

1: **if** $2f+1 \leq |S| < 3f+1$ **then**
2:    Client u sends $\texttt{Commit}(S)_u$ to all replicas
3:    Each replica r replies with a $\texttt{LocalCommit}(S)_r$ message to u
4:    Client u collects at least $2f+1$ $\texttt{LocalCommit}(S)_r$ messages and considers c to be complete
5: **end if**

Remarks:

- If replicas fail, a client u may receive less than $3f+1$ consistent responses from the replicas. Client u can only assume command c to be complete if all correct replicas r eventually append command c to their local history h^r.

Definition 5.10 (Commit Certificate). *A commit certificate S contains $2f+1$ consistent and signed $\text{Response}(a,\text{OR})_r$ messages from $2f+1$ different replicas r.*

Remarks:

- The set S is a commit certificate which proves the execution of the command on $2f+1$ replicas, of which at least $f+1$ are correct. This commit certificate S must be acknowledged by $2f+1$ replicas before the client considers the command to be complete.

- Why do clients have to distribute this commit certificate to $2f+1$ replicas? We will discuss this in Theorem 5.21.

- What if $|S| < 2f+1$, or what if the client receives $2f+1$ messages but some have inconsistent histories? Since at most f replicas are byzantine, the primary itself must be byzantine! Can we resolve this?

Byzantine Primary

Definition 5.11 (Proof of Misbehavior). *Proof of misbehavior of some node can be established by a set of contradicting signed messages.*

Remarks:

- For example, if a client u receives two $\text{Response}(a,\text{OR})_r$ messages that contain inconsistent OR messages signed by the primary, client u can prove that the primary misbehaved. Client u broadcasts this proof of misbehavior to all replicas r which initiate a view change by broadcasting a IHatePrimary_r message to all replicas.

5.2. ZYZZYVA

Algorithm 5.12 Zyzzyva: Byzantine Primary (append to Algorithm 5.9)

1: **if** $|S| < 2f + 1$ **then**
2:     Client u sends the original R = Request$(c,t)_u$ to all replicas
3:     Each replica r sends a ConfirmRequest(R)$_r$ message to p
4:     **if** primary p replies with OR **then**
5:         Replica r forwards OR to all replicas
6:         Continue as in Algorithm 5.8, Line 5
7:     **else**
8:         Replica r initiates view change by broadcasting IHatePrimary$_r$ to all replicas
9:     **end if**
10: **end if**

Remarks:

- A faulty primary can slow down Zyzzyva by not sending out the OrderedRequest messages in Algorithm 5.8, repeatedly escalating to Algorithm 5.12.

- Line 5 in the Algorithm is necessary to ensure liveness. We will discuss this in Theorem 5.27.

- Again, there is potential for optimization. For example, a replica might already know about a command that is requested by a client. In that case, it can answer without asking the primary. Furthermore, the primary might already know the message R requested by the replicas. In that case, it sends the old OR message to the requesting replica.

Safety

Definition 5.13 (Safety). *We call a system safe if the following condition holds: If a command with sequence number j and a history h_j completes, then for any command that completed earlier (with a smaller sequence number $i < j$), the history h_i is a prefix of history h_j.*

Remarks:

- In Zyzzyva a command can only complete in two ways, either in Algorithm 5.8 or in Algorithm 5.9.

- If a system is safe, complete commands cannot be reordered or dropped. So is Zyzzyva so far safe?

Lemma 5.14. *Let c_i and c_j be two different complete commands. Then c_i and c_j must have different sequence numbers.*

Proof. If a command c completes in Algorithm 5.8, $3f + 1$ replicas sent a Response$(a,\texttt{OR})_r$ to the client. If the command c completed in Algorithm 5.9, at least $2f + 1$ replicas sent a Response$(a,\texttt{OR})_r$ message to the client. Hence, a client has to receive at least $2f + 1$ Response$(a,\texttt{OR})_r$ messages.

Both c_i and c_j are complete. Therefore there must be at least $2f + 1$ replicas that responded to c_i with a Response$(a,\texttt{OR})_r$ message. But there are also at least $2f + 1$ replicas that responded to c_j with a Response$(a,\texttt{OR})_r$ message. Because there are only $3f + 1$ replicas, there is at least one correct replica that sent a Response$(a,\texttt{OR})_r$ message for both c_i and c_j. A correct replica only sends one Response$(a,\texttt{OR})_r$ message for each sequence number, hence the two commands must have different sequence numbers. □

Lemma 5.15. *Let c_i and c_j be two complete commands with sequence numbers $i < j$. The history h_i is a prefix of h_j.*

Proof. As in the proof of Lemma 5.14, there has to be at least one correct replica that sent a Response$(a,\texttt{OR})_r$ message for both c_i and c_j.

A correct replica r that sent a Response$(a,\texttt{OR})_r$ message for c_i will only accept c_j if the history for c_j provided by the primary is consistent with the local history of replica r, including c_i. □

Remarks:

- A byzantine primary can cause the system to never complete any command. Either by never sending any messages or by inconsistently ordering client requests. In this case, replicas have to replace the primary.

View Changes

Definition 5.16 (View Change). *In Zyzzyva, a view change is used to replace a byzantine primary with another (hopefully correct) replica. View changes are initiated by replicas sending* IHatePrimary$_r$ *to all other replicas. This only happens if a replica obtains a valid proof of misbehavior from a client or after a replica fails to obtain an* OR *message from the primary in Algorithm 5.12.*

Remarks:

- How can we safely decide to initiate a view change, i.e. demote a byzantine primary? Note that byzantine nodes should not be able to trigger a view change!

Algorithm 5.17 Zyzzyva: View Change Agreement

1: All replicas continuously collect the set H of IHatePrimary$_r$ messages
2: **if** a replica r received $|H| > f$ messages or a valid ViewChange message **then**
3:     Replica r broadcasts ViewChange(H^r,h^r,S_l^r)$_r$
4:     Replica r stops participating in the current view
5:     Replica r switches to the next primary "$p = p + 1$"
6: **end if**

Remarks:

- The $f+1$ IHatePrimary$_r$ messages in set H prove that at least one correct replica initiated a view change. This proof is broadcast to all replicas to make sure that once the first correct replica stopped acting in the current view, all other replicas will do so as well.

- S_l^r is the most recent commit certificate that the replica obtained in the ending view as described in Algorithm 5.9. S_l^r will be used to recover the correct history before the new view starts. The local histories h^r are included in the ViewChange(H^r,h^r,S_l^r)$_r$ message such that commands that completed after a correct client received $3f+1$ responses from replicas can be recovered as well.

- In Zyzzyva, a byzantine primary starts acting as a normal replica after a view change. In practice, all machines eventually break and rarely fix themselves after that. Instead, one could consider to replace a byzantine primary with a fresh replica that was not in the previous view.

Algorithm 5.18 Zyzzyva: View Change Execution

1: The new primary p collects the set C of ViewChange$(H^r, h^r, S_l^r)_r$ messages
2: **if** new primary p collected $|C| \geq 2f+1$ messages **then**
3:    New primary p sends NewView$(C)_p$ to all replicas
4: **end if**

5: **if** a replica r received a NewView$(C)_p$ message **then**
6:    Replica r recovers new history h_{new} as shown in Algorithm 5.20
7:    Replica r broadcasts ViewConfirm$(h_{\text{new}})_r$ message to all replicas
8: **end if**

9: **if** a replica r received $2f+1$ ViewConfirm$(h_{\text{new}})_r$ messages **then**
10:    Replica r accepts $h^r = h_{\text{new}}$ as the history of the new view
11:    Replica r starts participating in the new view
12: **end if**

Remarks:

- Analogously to Lemma 5.15, commit certificates are ordered. For two commit certificates S_i and S_j with sequence numbers $i < j$, the history h_i certified by S_i is a prefix of the history h_j certified by S_j.

- Zyzzyva collects the most recent commit certificate and the local history of $2f+1$ replicas. This information is distributed to all replicas, and used to recover the history for the new view h_{new}.

- If a replica does not receive the NewView$(C)_p$ or the ViewConfirm$(h_{\text{new}})_r$ message in time, it triggers another view change by broadcasting IHatePrimary$_r$ to all other replicas.

- How is the history recovered exactly? It seems that the set of histories included in C can be messy. How can

5.2. ZYZZYVA

we be sure that complete commands are not reordered or dropped?

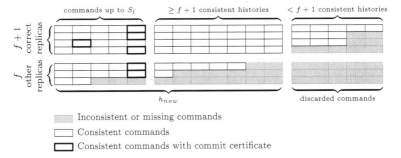

Figure 5.19: The structure of the data reported by different replicas in C. Commands up to the last commit certificate S_l were completed in either Algorithm 5.8 or Algorithm 5.9. After the last commit certificate S_l there may be commands that completed at a correct client in Algorithm 5.8. Algorithm 5.20 shows how the new history h_{new} is recovered such that no complete commands are lost.

Algorithm 5.20 Zyzzyva: History Recovery

1: C = set of $2f + 1$ ViewChange$(H^r, h^r, S^r)_r$ messages in NewView$(C)_p$
2: R = set of replicas included in C
3: S_l = most recent commit certificate S_l^r reported in C
4: $h_{\texttt{new}}$ = history h_l contained in S_l
5: $k = l + 1$, next sequence number
6: **while** command c_k exists in C **do**
7:    **if** c_k is reported by at least $f + 1$ replicas in R **then**
8:       Remove replicas from R that do not support c_k
9:       $h_{\texttt{new}} = (h_{\texttt{new}}, c_k)$
10:    **end if**
11:    $k = k + 1$
12: **end while**
13: **return** $h_{\texttt{new}}$

56 CHAPTER 5. AUTHENTICATED AGREEMENT

Remarks:

- Commands up to S_l are included into the new history h_{new}.

- If at least $f + 1$ replicas share a consistent history after the last commit certificate S_l, also the commands after that are included.

- Even if $f + 1$ correct replicas consistently report a command c after the last commit certificate S_l, c may not be considered complete by a client, e.g., because one of the responses to the client was lost. Such a command is included in the new history h_{new}. When the client retries executing c, the replicas will be able to identify the same command c using the timestamp included in the client's request, and avoid duplicate execution of the command.

- Can we be sure that all commands that completed at a correct client are carried over into the new view?

Lemma 5.21. *The globally most recent commit certificate S_l is included in C.*

Proof. Any two sets of $2f + 1$ replicas share at least one correct replica. Hence, at least one correct replica which acknowledged the most recent commit certificate S_l also sent a $\texttt{LocalCommit}(S_l)_r$ message that is in C. □

Lemma 5.22. *Any command and its history that completes after S_l has to be reported in C at least $f + 1$ times.*

Proof. A command c can only complete in Algorithm 5.8 after S_l. Hence, $3f + 1$ replicas sent a $\texttt{Response}(a,\texttt{OR})_r$ message for c. C includes the local histories of $2f + 1$ replicas of which at most f are byzantine. As a result, c and its history is consistently found in at least $f + 1$ local histories in C. □

Lemma 5.23. *If a command c is considered complete by a client, command c remains in its place in the history during view changes.*

Proof. We have shown in Lemma 5.21 that the most recent commit certificate is contained in C, and hence any command that terminated in Algorithm 5.9 is included in the new history after a view change. Every command that completed before the last commit certificate S_l is included in the history as a result. Commands that

5.2. ZYZZYVA

completed in Algorithm 5.8 after the last commit certificate are supported by at least $f+1$ correct replicas as shown in Lemma 5.22. Such commands are added to the new history as described in Algorithm 5.20. Algorithm 5.20 adds commands sequentially until the histories become inconsistent. Hence, complete commands are not lost or reordered during a view change. □

Theorem 5.24. *Zyzzyva is safe even during view changes.*

Proof. Complete commands are not reordered within a view as described in Lemma 5.15. Also, no complete command is lost or reordered during a view change as shown in Lemma 5.23. Hence, Zyzzyva is safe. □

Remarks:

- So Zyzzyva correctly handles complete commands even in the presence of failures. We also want Zyzzyva to make progress, i.e., commands issued by correct clients should complete eventually.

- If the network is broken or introduces arbitrarily large delays, commands may never complete.

- Can we be sure commands complete in periods in which delays are bounded?

Definition 5.25 (Liveness). *We call a system **live** if every command eventually completes.*

Lemma 5.26. *Zyzzyva is live during periods of synchrony if the primary is correct and a command is requested by a correct client.*

Proof. The client receives a $\texttt{Response}(a,\texttt{OR})_r$ message from all correct replicas. If it receives $3f+1$ messages, the command completes immediately in Algorithm 5.8. If the client receives fewer than $3f+1$ messages, it will at least receive $2f+1$, since there are at most f byzantine replicas. All correct replicas will answer the client's $\texttt{Commit}(S)_u$ message with a correct $\texttt{LocalCommit}(S)_r$ message after which the command completes in Algorithm 5.9. □

Lemma 5.27. *If, during a period of synchrony, a request does not complete in Algorithm 5.8 or Algorithm 5.9, a view change occurs.*

Proof. If a command does not complete for a sufficiently long time, the client will resend the $\text{R} = \text{Request}(c,t)_u$ message to all replicas. After that, if a replica's $\text{ConfirmRequest}(\text{R})_r$ message is not answered in time by the primary, it broadcasts an IHatePrimary_r message. If a correct replica gathers $f+1$ IHatePrimary_r messages, the view change is initiated. If no correct replica collects more than f IHatePrimary_r messages, at least one correct replica received a valid $\text{OrderedRequest}(h^p, c, \text{R})_p$ message from the primary which it forwards to all other replicas. In that case, the client is guaranteed to receive at least $2f+1$ $\text{Response}(a,\text{OR})_r$ messages from the correct replicas and can complete the command by assembling a commit certificate. □

Remarks:

- If the newly elected primary is byzantine, the view change may never terminate. However, we can detect if the new primary does not assemble C correctly as all contained messages are signed. If the primary refuses to assemble C, replicas initiate another view change after a timeout.

Chapter Notes

Algorithm 5.2 was introduced by Dolev et al. [DFF+82] in 1982. Byzantine fault tolerant state machine replication (BFT) is a problem that gave rise to various protocols. Castro and Liskov [MC99] introduced the Practical Byzantine Fault Tolerance (PBFT) protocol in 1999, applications such as Farsite [ABC+02] followed. This triggered the development of, e.g., Q/U [AEMGG+05] and HQ [CML+06]. Zyzzyva [KAD+07] improved on performance especially in the case of no failures, while Aardvark [CWA+09] improved performance in the presence of failures. Guerraoui at al. [GKQV10] introduced a modular system which allows to more easily develop BFT protocols that match specific applications in terms of robustness or best case performance.

Bibliography

[ABC+02] Atul Adya, William J. Bolosky, Miguel Castro, Gerald Cermak, Ronnie Chaiken, John R. Douceur, Jon Howell, Jacob R. Lorch, Marvin Theimer,

BIBLIOGRAPHY 59

and Roger P. Wattenhofer. Farsite: Federated, available, and reliable storage for an incompletely trusted environment. *SIGOPS Oper. Syst. Rev.*, 36(SI):1–14, December 2002.

[AEMGG+05] Michael Abd-El-Malek, Gregory R Ganger, Garth R Goodson, Michael K Reiter, and Jay J Wylie. Fault-scalable byzantine fault-tolerant services. *ACM SIGOPS Operating Systems Review*, 39(5):59–74, 2005.

[CML+06] James Cowling, Daniel Myers, Barbara Liskov, Rodrigo Rodrigues, and Liuba Shrira. Hq replication: A hybrid quorum protocol for byzantine fault tolerance. In *Proceedings of the 7th Symposium on Operating Systems Design and Implementation*, OSDI '06, pages 177–190, Berkeley, CA, USA, 2006. USENIX Association.

[CWA+09] Allen Clement, Edmund L Wong, Lorenzo Alvisi, Michael Dahlin, and Mirco Marchetti. Making byzantine fault tolerant systems tolerate byzantine faults. In *NSDI*, volume 9, pages 153–168, 2009.

[DFF+82] Danny Dolev, Michael J Fischer, Rob Fowler, Nancy A Lynch, and H Raymond Strong. An efficient algorithm for byzantine agreement without authentication. *Information and Control*, 52(3):257–274, 1982.

[GKQV10] Rachid Guerraoui, Nikola Knežević, Vivien Quéma, and Marko Vukolić. The next 700 bft protocols. In *Proceedings of the 5th European conference on Computer systems*, pages 363–376. ACM, 2010.

[KAD+07] Ramakrishna Kotla, Lorenzo Alvisi, Mike Dahlin, Allen Clement, and Edmund Wong. Zyzzyva: speculative byzantine fault tolerance. In *ACM SIGOPS Operating Systems Review*, volume 41, pages 45–58. ACM, 2007.

[MC99] Barbara Liskov Miguel Castro. Practical byzantine fault tolerance. In *OSDI*, volume 99, pages 173–186, 1999.

Chapter 6

Quorum Systems

What happens if a single server is no longer powerful enough to service all your customers? The obvious choice is to add more servers and to use the majority approach (e.g. Paxos, Chapter 2) to guarantee consistency. However, even if you buy one million servers, a client still has to access more than half of them per request! While you gain fault-tolerance, your efficiency can at most be doubled. Do we have to give up on consistency?

Let us take a step back: We used majorities because majority sets always overlap. But are majority sets the only sets that guarantee overlap? In this chapter we study the theory behind overlapping sets, known as quorum systems.

Definition 6.1 (quorum, quorum system)**.** *Let $V = \{v_1, \ldots, v_n\}$ be a set of nodes. A **quorum** $Q \subseteq V$ is a subset of these nodes. A **quorum system** $\mathcal{S} \subset 2^V$ is a set of quorums s.t. every two quorums intersect, i.e., $Q_1 \cap Q_2 \neq \emptyset$ for all $Q_1, Q_2 \in \mathcal{S}$.*

Remarks:

- When a quorum system is being used, a client selects a quorum, acquires a lock (or ticket) on all nodes of the quorum, and when done releases all locks again. The idea is that no matter which quorum is chosen, its nodes will intersect with the nodes of every other quorum.

- What can happen if two quorums try to lock their nodes at the same time?

- A quorum system $\mathcal{S}$ is called **minimal** if $\forall Q_1, Q_2 \in \mathcal{S} : Q_1 \not\subset Q_2$.

- The simplest quorum system imaginable consists of just one quorum, which in turn just consists of one server. It is known as **Singleton**.

- In the **Majority** quorum system, every quorum has $\lfloor \frac{n}{2} \rfloor + 1$ nodes.

- Can you think of other simple quorum systems?

6.1 Load and Work

Definition 6.2 (access strategy). *An **access strategy** Z defines the probability $P_Z(Q)$ of accessing a quorum $Q \in \mathcal{S}$ s.t. $\sum_{Q \in \mathcal{S}} P_Z(Q) = 1$.*

Definition 6.3 (load).

- *The **load** of access strategy Z on a node v_i is $L_Z(v_i) = \sum_{Q \in \mathcal{S}; v_i \in Q} P_Z(Q)$.*

- *The **load** induced by access strategy Z on a quorum system $\mathcal{S}$ is the maximal load induced by Z on any node in $\mathcal{S}$, i.e., $L_Z(\mathcal{S}) = \max_{v_i \in \mathcal{S}} L_Z(v_i)$.*

- *The **load** of a quorum system $\mathcal{S}$ is $L(\mathcal{S}) = \min_Z L_Z(\mathcal{S})$.*

Definition 6.4 (work).

- *The **work** of a quorum $Q \in \mathcal{S}$ is the number of nodes in Q, $W(Q) = |Q|$.*

- *The **work** induced by access strategy Z on a quorum system $\mathcal{S}$ is the expected number of nodes accessed, i.e., $W_Z(\mathcal{S}) = \sum_{Q \in \mathcal{S}} P_Z(Q) \cdot W(Q)$.*

- *The **work** of a quorum system $\mathcal{S}$ is $W(\mathcal{S}) = \min_Z W_Z(\mathcal{S})$.*

Remarks:

- Note that you cannot choose different access strategies Z for work and load, you have to pick a single Z for both.

- We illustrate the above concepts with a small example. Let $V = \{v_1, v_2, v_3, v_4, v_5\}$ and $\mathcal{S} = \{Q_1, Q_2, Q_3, Q_4\}$, with $Q_1 = \{v_1, v_2\}$, $Q_2 = \{v_1, v_3, v_4\}$, $Q_3 = \{v_2, v_3, v_5\}$, $Q_4 = \{v_2, v_4, v_5\}$. If we choose the access strategy Z

6.1. LOAD AND WORK

s.t. $P_Z(Q_1) = 1/2$ and $P_Z(Q_2) = P_Z(Q_3) = P_Z(Q_4) = 1/6$, then the node with the highest load is v_2 with $L_Z(v_2) = 1/2 + 1/6 + 1/6 = 5/6$, i.e., $L_Z(S) = 5/6$. Regarding work, we have $W_Z(S) = 1/2 \cdot 2 + 1/6 \cdot 3 + 1/6 \cdot 3 + 1/6 \cdot 3 = 15/6$.

- Can you come up with a better access strategy for S?

- If every quorum Q in a quorum system S has the same number of elements, S is called *uniform*.

- What is the minimum load a quorum system can have?

Primary Copy vs. Majority		Singleton	Majority
How many nodes need to be accessed?	(Work)	1	$> n/2$
What is the load of the busiest node?	(Load)	1	$> 1/2$

Table 6.5: First comparison of the Singleton and Majority quorum systems. Note that the Singleton quorum system can be a good choice when the failure probability of every single node is $> 1/2$.

Theorem 6.6. *Let S be a quorum system. Then $L(S) \geq 1/\sqrt{n}$ holds.*

Proof. Let $Q = \{v_1, \ldots, v_q\}$ be a quorum of minimal size in S, with sizes $|Q| = q$ and $|S| = s$. Let Z be an access strategy for S. Every other quorum in S intersects in at least one element with this quorum Q. Each time a quorum is accessed, at least one node in Q is accessed as well, yielding a lower bound of $L_Z(v_i) \geq 1/q$ for some $v_i \in Q$.

Furthermore, as Q is minimal, at least q nodes need to be accessed, yielding $W(S) \geq q$. Thus, $L_Z(v_i) \geq q/n$ for some $v_i \in Q$, as each time q nodes are accessed, the load of the most accessed node is at least q/n.

Combining both ideas leads to $L_Z(S) \geq \max(1/q, q/n) \Rightarrow L_Z(S) \geq 1/\sqrt{n}$. Thus, $L(S) \geq 1/\sqrt{n}$, as Z can be *any* access strategy. □

Remarks:

- Can we achieve this load?

6.2 Grid Quorum Systems

Definition 6.7 (Basic Grid quorum system). *Assume $\sqrt{n} \in \mathbb{N}$, and arrange the n nodes in a square matrix with side length of $\sqrt{n}$, i.e., in a grid. The basic **Grid** quorum system consists of $\sqrt{n}$ quorums, with each containing the full row i and the full column i, for $1 \leq i \leq \sqrt{n}$.*

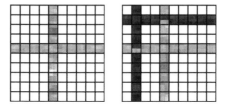

Figure 6.8: The basic version of the Grid quorum system, where each quorum Q_i with $1 \leq i \leq \sqrt{n}$ uses row i and column i. The size of each quorum is $2\sqrt{n}-1$ and two quorums overlap in exactly two nodes. Thus, when the access strategy Z is uniform (i.e., the probability of each quorum is $1/\sqrt{n}$), the work is $2\sqrt{n}-1$, and the load of every node is in $\Theta(1/\sqrt{n})$.

Remarks:

- Consider the right picture in Figure 6.8: The two quorums intersect in two nodes. If both quorums were to be accessed at the same time, it is not guaranteed that at least one quorum will lock all of its nodes, as they could enter a deadlock!

- In the case of just two quorums, one could solve this by letting the quorums just intersect in one node, see Figure 6.9. However, already with three quorums the same situation could occur again, progress is not guaranteed!

- However, by deviating from the "access all at once" strategy, we can guarantee progress if the nodes are totally ordered!

Theorem 6.11. *If each quorum is accessed by Algorithm 6.10, at least one quorum will obtain a lock for all of its nodes.*

Proof. We prove the theorem by contradiction. Assume no quorum can make progress, i.e., for every quorum we have: At least one of

6.2. GRID QUORUM SYSTEMS

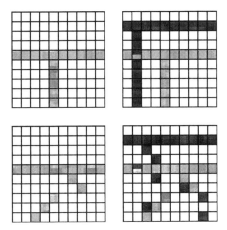

Figure 6.9: There are other ways to choose quorums in the grid s.t. pairwise different quorums only intersect in one node. The size of each quorum is between $\sqrt{n}$ and $2\sqrt{n} - 1$, i.e., the work is in $\Theta(\sqrt{n})$. When the access strategy Z is uniform, the load of every node is in $\Theta(1/\sqrt{n})$.

Algorithm 6.10 Sequential Locking Strategy for a Quorum Q

1: Attempt to lock the nodes one by one, ordered by their identifiers
2: Should a node be already locked, release all locks and start over
---

its nodes is locked by another quorum. Let v be the node with the highest identifier that is locked by some quorum Q. Observe that Q already locked all of its nodes with a smaller identifier than v, otherwise Q would have restarted. As all nodes with a higher identifier than v are not locked, Q either has locked all of its nodes or can make progress – a contradiction. As the set of nodes is finite, one quorum will eventually be able to lock all of its nodes. □

Remarks:

- But now we are back to sequential accesses in a distributed system? Let's do it concurrently with the same idea, i.e., resolving conflicts by the ordering of the nodes. Then, a quorum that locked the highest identifier so far can always make progress!

Algorithm 6.12 Concurrent Locking Strategy for a Quorum Q

Invariant: Let $v_Q \in Q$ be the highest identifier of a node locked by Q s.t. all nodes $v_i \in Q$ with $v_i < v_Q$ are locked by Q as well. Should Q not have any lock, then v_Q is set to 0.

1: **repeat**
2:    Attempt to lock all nodes of the quorum Q
3:    **for each** node $v \in Q$ that was not able to be locked by Q **do**
4:       exchange v_Q and $v_{Q'}$ with the quorum Q' that locked v
5:       **if** $v_Q > v_{Q'}$ **then**
6:          Q' releases lock on v and Q acquires lock on v
7:       **end if**
8:    **end for**
9: **until** all nodes of the quorum Q are locked

Theorem 6.13. *If the nodes and quorums use Algorithm 6.12, at least one quorum will obtain a lock for all of its nodes.*

Proof. The proof is analogous to the proof of Theorem 6.11: Assume for contradiction that no quorum can make progress. However, at least the quorum with the highest v_Q can always make progress – a contradiction! As the set of nodes is finite, at least one quorum will eventually be able to acquire a lock on all of its nodes. □

Remarks:

- What if a quorum locks all of its nodes and then crashes? Is the quorum system dead now? This issue can be prevented by, e.g., using leases instead of locks: leases have a timeout, i.e., a lock is released eventually.

6.3 Fault Tolerance

Definition 6.14 (resilience). *If any f nodes from a quorum system S can fail s.t. there is still a quorum $Q \in S$ without failed nodes, then S is f-resilient. The largest such f is the **resilience** $R(S)$.*

Theorem 6.15. *Let S be a Grid quorum system where each of the n quorums consists of a full row and a full column. S has a resilience of $\sqrt{n} - 1$.*

6.3. FAULT TOLERANCE

Proof. If all $\sqrt{n}$ nodes on the diagonal of the grid fail, then every quorum will have at least one failed node. Should less than $\sqrt{n}$ nodes fail, then there is a row and a column without failed nodes. □

Definition 6.16 (failure probability). *Assume that every node works with a fixed probability p (in the following we assume concrete values, e.g. $p > 1/2$). The **failure probability** $F_p(\mathcal{S})$ of a quorum system $\mathcal{S}$ is the probability that at least one node of every quorum fails.*

Remarks:

- The **asymptotic failure probability** is $F_p(\mathcal{S})$ for $n \to \infty$.

Facts 6.17. *A version of a **Chernoff bound** states the following: Let $x_1, \ldots, x_n$ be independent Bernoulli-distributed random variables with $Pr[x_i = 1] = p_i$ and $Pr[x_i = 0] = 1 - p_i = q_i$, then for $X := \sum_{i=1}^{n} x_i$ and $\mu := \mathbb{E}[X] = \sum_{i=1}^{n} p_i$ the following holds:*

for all $0 < \delta < 1$: $Pr[X \leq (1-\delta)\mu] \leq e^{-\mu\delta^2/2}$.

Theorem 6.18. *The asymptotic failure probability of the Majority quorum system is 0.*

Proof. In a Majority quorum system each quorum contains exactly $\lfloor \frac{n}{2} \rfloor + 1$ nodes and each subset of nodes with cardinality $\lfloor \frac{n}{2} \rfloor + 1$ forms a quorum. The Majority quorum system fails, if only $\lfloor \frac{n}{2} \rfloor$ nodes work. Otherwise there is at least one quorum available. In order to calculate the failure probability we define the following random variables:

$$x_i = \begin{cases} 1, & \text{if node } i \text{ works, happens with probability } p \\ 0, & \text{if node } i \text{ fails, happens with probability } q = 1 - p \end{cases}$$

and $X := \sum_{i=1}^{n} x_i$, with $\mu = np$,

whereas X corresponds to the number of working nodes. To estimate the probability that the number of working nodes is less than $\lfloor \frac{n}{2} \rfloor + 1$ we will make use of the Chernoff inequality from above. By setting $\delta = 1 - \frac{1}{2p}$ we obtain $F_P(\mathcal{S}) = Pr[X \leq \lfloor \frac{n}{2} \rfloor] \leq Pr[X \leq \frac{n}{2}] = Pr[X \leq (1-\delta)\mu]$.

With $\delta = 1 - \frac{1}{2p}$ we have $0 < \delta \leq 1/2$ due to $1/2 < p \leq 1$. Thus, we can use the Chernoff bound and get $F_P(\mathcal{S}) \leq e^{-\mu\delta^2/2} \in e^{-\Omega(n)}$. □

Theorem 6.19. *The asymptotic failure probability of the Grid quorum system is 1.*

Proof. Consider the $n = d \cdot d$ nodes to be arranged in a $d \times d$ grid. A quorum always contains one full row. In this estimation we will make use of the Bernoulli inequality which states that for all $n \in \mathbb{N}, x \geq -1 : (1 + x)^n \geq 1 + nx$.

The system fails, if in each row at least one node fails (which happens with probability $1 - p^d$ for a particular row, as all nodes work with probability p^d). Therefore we can bound the failure probability from below with:

$F_p(\mathcal{S}) \geq Pr[\text{at least one failure per row}] = (1 - p^d)^d \geq 1 - dp^d \xrightarrow[n \to \infty]{} 1.$ □

Remarks:

- Now we have a quorum system with optimal load (the Grid) and one with fault-tolerance (Majority), but what if we want both?

Definition 6.20 (B-Grid quorum system). *Consider $n = dhr$ nodes, arranged in a rectangular grid with $h \cdot r$ rows and d columns. Each group of r rows is a band, and r elements in a column restricted to a band are called a mini-column. A quorum consists of one mini-column in every band and one element from each mini-column of one band; thus every quorum has $d + hr - 1$ elements. The **B-Grid** quorum system consists of all such quorums.*

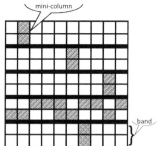

Figure 6.21: A B-Grid quorum system with $n = 100$ nodes, $d = 10$ columns, $h \cdot r = 10$ rows, $h = 5$ bands, and $r = 2$. The depicted quorum has a $d + hr - 1 = 10 + 5 \cdot 2 - 1 = 19$ nodes. If the access strategy Z is chosen uniformly, then we have a work of $d + hr - 1$ and a load of $\frac{d+hr-1}{n}$. By setting $d = \sqrt{n}$ and $r = \log n$, we obtain a work of $\Theta(\sqrt{n})$ and a load of $\Theta(1/\sqrt{n})$.

6.3. FAULT TOLERANCE

Theorem 6.22. *The asymptotic failure probability of the B-Grid quorum system is* 0.

Proof. Suppose $n = dhr$ and the elements are arranged in a grid with d columns and $h \cdot r$ rows. The B-Grid quorum system does fail if in each band a complete mini-column fails, because then it is not possible to choose a band where in each mini-column an element is still working. It also fails if in a band an element in each mini-column fails. Those events may not be independent of each other, but with the help of the union bound, we can upper bound the failure probability with the following equation:

$$F_p(\mathcal{S}) \leq Pr[\text{in every band a complete mini-column fails}]$$
$$+ Pr[\text{in a band at least one element of every m.-col. fails}]$$
$$\leq (d(1-p)^r)^h + h(1-p^r)^d$$

We use $d = \sqrt{n}, r = \ln d$, and $0 \leq (1-p) \leq 1/3$. Using $n^{\ln x} = x^{\ln n}$, we have $d(1-p)^r \leq d \cdot d^{\ln 1/3} \approx d^{-0.1}$, and hence for large enough d the whole first term is bounded from above by $d^{-0.1h} \ll 1/d^2 = 1/n$.

Regarding the second term, we have $p \geq 2/3$, and $h = d/\ln d < d$. Hence we can bound the term from above by $d(1 - d^{\ln 2/3})^d \approx d(1-d^{-0.4})^d$. Using $(1+t/n)^n \leq e^t$, we get (again, for large enough d) an upper bound of $d(1-d^{-0.4})^d = d(1-d^{0.6}/d)^d \leq d \cdot e^{-d^{0.6}} = d^{(-d^{0.6}/\ln d)+1} \ll d^{-2} = 1/n$. In total, we have $F_p(\mathcal{S}) \in O(1/n)$. □

	Singleton	Majority	Grid	B-Grid*
Work	1	$> n/2$	$\Theta(\sqrt{n})$	$\Theta(\sqrt{n})$
Load	1	$> 1/2$	$\Theta(1/\sqrt{n})$	$\Theta(1/\sqrt{n})$
Resilience	0	$< n/2$	$\Theta(\sqrt{n})$	$\Theta(\sqrt{n})$
F. Prob.**	$1-p$	$\to 0$	$\to 1$	$\to 0$

Table 6.23: Overview of the different quorum systems regarding resilience, work, load, and their asymptotic failure probability. The best entries in each row are set in bold.
* Setting $d = \sqrt{n}$ and $r = \log n$
** Assuming prob. $q = (1-p)$ is constant but significantly less than $1/2$

6.4 Byzantine Quorum Systems

While failed nodes are bad, they are still easy to deal with: just access another quorum where all nodes can respond! Byzantine nodes make life more difficult however, as they can pretend to be a regular node, i.e., one needs more sophisticated methods to deal with them. We need to ensure that the intersection of two quorums always contains a non-byzantine (correct) node and furthermore, the byzantine nodes should not be allowed to infiltrate every quorum. In this section we study three counter-measures of increasing strength, and their implications on the load of quorum systems.

Definition 6.24 (f-disseminating)**.** *A quorum system $\mathcal{S}$ is f-disseminating if (1) the intersection of two different quorums always contains $f + 1$ nodes, and (2) for any set of f byzantine nodes, there is at least one quorum without byzantine nodes.*

Remarks:

- Thanks to (2), even with f byzantine nodes, the byzantine nodes cannot stop all quorums by just pretending to have crashed. At least one quorum will survive. We will also keep this assumption for the upcoming more advanced byzantine quorum systems.

- Byzantine nodes can also do something worse than crashing - they could falsify data! Nonetheless, due to (1), there is at least one non-byzantine node in every quorum intersection. If the data is self-verifying by, e.g., authentication, then this one node is enough.

- If the data is not self-verifying, then we need another mechanism.

Definition 6.25 (f-masking)**.** *A quorum system $\mathcal{S}$ is f-masking if (1) the intersection of two different quorums always contains $2f + 1$ nodes, and (2) for any set of f byzantine nodes, there is at least one quorum without byzantine nodes.*

Remarks:

- Note that except for the second condition, an f-masking quorum system is the same as a $2f$-disseminating system. The idea is that the non-byzantine nodes (at least $f + 1$) can outvote the byzantine ones (at most f), but only if all non-byzantine nodes are up-to-date!

6.4. BYZANTINE QUORUM SYSTEMS

- This raises an issue not covered yet in this chapter. If we access some quorum and update its values, this change still has to be disseminated to the other nodes in the byzantine quorum system. Opaque quorum systems deal with this issue, which are discussed at the end of this section.

- f-disseminating quorum systems need more than $3f$ nodes and f-masking quorum systems need more than $4f$ nodes. Essentially, the quorums may not contain too many nodes, and the different intersection properties lead to the different bounds.

Theorem 6.26. *Let $\mathcal{S}$ be a f-disseminating quorum system. Then $L(\mathcal{S}) \geq \sqrt{(f+1)/n}$ holds.*

Theorem 6.27. *Let $\mathcal{S}$ be a f-masking quorum system. Then $L(\mathcal{S}) \geq \sqrt{(2f+1)/n}$ holds.*

Proofs of Theorems 6.26 and 6.27. The proofs follow the proof of Theorem 6.6, by observing that now not just one element is accessed from a minimal quorum, but $f+1$ or $2f+1$, respectively. □

Definition 6.28 (f-masking Grid quorum system)**.** *A f-masking Grid quorum system is constructed as the grid quorum system, but each quorum contains one full column and $f+1$ rows of nodes, with $2f+1 \leq \sqrt{n}$.*

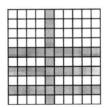

Figure 6.29: An example how to choose a quorum in the f-masking Grid with $f = 2$, i.e., $2+1 = 3$ rows. The load is in $\Theta(f/\sqrt{n})$ when the access strategy is chosen to be uniform. Two quorums overlap by their columns intersecting each other's rows, i.e., they overlap in at least $2f + 2$ nodes.

Remarks:

- The f-masking Grid nearly hits the lower bound for the load of f-masking quorum systems, but not quite. A small change and we will be optimal asymptotically.

Definition 6.30 (M-Grid quorum system). *The **M-Grid** quorum system is constructed as the grid quorum as well, but each quorum contains $\sqrt{f+1}$ rows and $\sqrt{f+1}$ columns of nodes, with $f \leq \frac{\sqrt{n}-1}{2}$.*

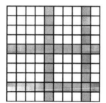

Figure 6.31: An example how to choose a quorum in the M-Grid with $f = 3$, i.e., 2 rows and 2 columns. The load is in $\Theta(\sqrt{f/n})$ when the access strategy is chosen to be uniform. Two quorums overlap with each row intersecting each other's column, i.e., $2\sqrt{f+1}^2 = 2f + 2$ nodes.

Corollary 6.32. *The f-masking Grid quorum system and the M-Grid quorum system are f-masking quorum systems.*

Remarks:

- We achieved nearly the same load as without byzantine nodes! However, as mentioned earlier, what happens if we access a quorum that is not up-to-date, except for the intersection with an up-to-date quorum? Surely we can fix that as well without too much loss?

- This property will be handled in the last part of this chapter by *opaque* quorum systems. It will ensure that the number of correct up-to-date nodes accessed will be larger than the number of out-of-date nodes combined with the byzantine nodes in the quorum (cf. (6.33.1)).

6.4. BYZANTINE QUORUM SYSTEMS

Definition 6.33 (*f*-opaque quorum system). *A quorum system S is f-**opaque** if the following two properties hold for any set of f byzantine nodes F and any two different quorums Q_1, Q_2:*

$$|(Q_1 \cap Q_2) \setminus F| > |(Q_2 \cap F) \cup (Q_2 \setminus Q_1)| \qquad (6.33.1)$$

$$(F \cap Q) = \emptyset \text{ for some } Q \in S \qquad (6.33.2)$$

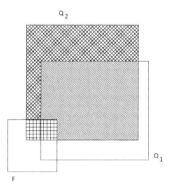

Figure 6.34: Intersection properties of an opaque quorum system. Equation (6.33.1) ensures that the set of non-byzantine nodes in the intersection of Q_1, Q_2 is larger than the set of out of date nodes, even if the byzantine nodes "team up" with those nodes. Thus, the correct up to date value can always be recognized by a majority voting.

Theorem 6.35. *Let S be a f-opaque quorum system. Then, $n > 5f$.*

Proof. Due to (6.33.2), there exists a quorum Q_1 with size at most $n - f$. With (6.33.1), $|Q_1| > f$ holds. Let F_1 be a set of f (byzantine) nodes $F_1 \subset Q_1$, and with (6.33.2), there exists a $Q_2 \subset V \setminus F_1$. Thus, $|Q_1 \cap Q_2| \leq n - 2f$. With (6.33.1), $|Q_1 \cap Q_2| > f$ holds. Thus, one could choose f (byzantine) nodes F_2 with $F_2 \subset (Q_1 \cap Q_2)$. Using (6.33.1) one can bound $n - 3f$ from below: $n - 3f > |(Q_2 \cap Q_1)| - |F_2| \geq |(Q_2 \cap Q_1) \cup (Q_1 \cap F_2)| \geq |F_1| + |F_2| = 2f$. $\square$

Remarks:

- One can extend the Majority quorum system to be f-opaque by setting the size of each quorum to contain $\lceil (2n+2f)/3 \rceil$ nodes. Then its load is $1/n \lceil (2n+2f)/3 \rceil \approx 2/3 + 2f/3n \geq 2/3$.

- Can we do much better? Sadly, no...

Theorem 6.36. *Let $\mathcal{S}$ be a f-opaque quorum system. Then $L(\mathcal{S}) \geq 1/2$ holds.*

Proof. Equation (6.33.1) implies that for $Q_1, Q_2 \in \mathcal{S}$, the intersection of both Q_1, Q_2 is at least half their size, i.e., $|(Q_1 \cap Q_2)| \geq |Q_1|/2$. Let $\mathcal{S}$ consist of quorums $Q_1, Q_2, \ldots$. The load induced by an access strategy Z on Q_1 is:

$$\sum_{v \in Q_1} \sum_{v \in Q_i} L_Z(Q_i) \geq \sum_{Q_i} (|Q_1|/2) \, L_Z(Q_i) = |Q_1|/2 \, .$$

Using the pigeonhole principle, there must be at least one node in Q_1 with load of at least $1/2$. □

Chapter Notes

Historically, a quorum is the minimum number of members of a deliberative body necessary to conduct the business of that group. Their use has inspired the introduction of quorum systems in computer science since the late 1970s/early 1980s. Early work focused on Majority quorum systems [Lam78, Gif79, Tho79], with the notion of minimality introduced shortly after [GB85]. The Grid quorum system was first considered in [Mae85], with the B-Grid being introduced in [NW94]. The latter article and [PW95] also initiated the study of load and resilience.

The f-masking Grid quorum system and opaque quorum systems are from [MR98], and the M-Grid quorum system was introduced in [MRW97]. Both papers also mark the start of the formal study of Byzantine quorum systems. The f-masking and the M-Grid have asymptotic failure probabilities of 1, more complex systems with better values can be found in these papers as well.

Quorum systems have also been extended to cope with nodes dynamically leaving and joining, see, e.g., the dynamic paths quorum system in [NW05].

For a further overview on quorum systems, we refer to the book by Vukolić [Vuk12] and the article by Merideth and Reiter [MR10].

Bibliography

[GB85] Hector Garcia-Molina and Daniel Barbará. How to assign votes in a distributed system. *J. ACM*, 32(4):841–860, 1985.

[Gif79] David K. Gifford. Weighted voting for replicated data. In Michael D. Schroeder and Anita K. Jones, editors, *Proceedings of the Seventh Symposium on Operating System Principles, SOSP 1979, Asilomar Conference Grounds, Pacific Grove, California, USA, 10-12, December 1979*, pages 150–162. ACM, 1979.

[Lam78] Leslie Lamport. The implementation of reliable distributed multiprocess systems. *Computer Networks*, 2:95–114, 1978.

[Mae85] Mamoru Maekawa. A square root N algorithm for mutual exclusion in decentralized systems. *ACM Trans. Comput. Syst.*, 3(2):145–159, 1985.

[MR98] Dahlia Malkhi and Michael K. Reiter. Byzantine quorum systems. *Distributed Computing*, 11(4):203–213, 1998.

[MR10] Michael G. Merideth and Michael K. Reiter. Selected results from the latest decade of quorum systems research. In Bernadette Charron-Bost, Fernando Pedone, and André Schiper, editors, *Replication: Theory and Practice*, volume 5959 of *Lecture Notes in Computer Science*, pages 185–206. Springer, 2010.

[MRW97] Dahlia Malkhi, Michael K. Reiter, and Avishai Wool. The load and availability of byzantine quorum systems. In James E. Burns and Hagit Attiya, editors, *Proceedings of the Sixteenth Annual ACM Symposium on Principles of Distributed Computing, Santa Barbara, California, USA, August 21-24, 1997*, pages 249–257. ACM, 1997.

[NW94] Moni Naor and Avishai Wool. The load, capacity and availability of quorum systems. In *35th Annual Symposium on Foundations of Computer Science, Santa Fe,*

New Mexico, USA, 20-22 November 1994, pages 214–225. IEEE Computer Society, 1994.

[NW05] Moni Naor and Udi Wieder. Scalable and dynamic quorum systems. *Distributed Computing*, 17(4):311–322, 2005.

[PW95] David Peleg and Avishai Wool. The availability of quorum systems. *Inf. Comput.*, 123(2):210–223, 1995.

[Tho79] Robert H. Thomas. A majority consensus approach to concurrency control for multiple copy databases. *ACM Trans. Database Syst.*, 4(2):180–209, 1979.

[Vuk12] Marko Vukolic. *Quorum Systems: With Applications to Storage and Consensus*. Synthesis Lectures on Distributed Computing Theory. Morgan & Claypool Publishers, 2012.

Chapter 7

Eventual Consistency & Bitcoin

How would you implement an ATM? Does the following implementation work satisfactorily?

Algorithm 7.1 Naïve ATM

1: ATM makes withdrawal request to bank
2: ATM waits for response from bank
3: **if** balance of customer sufficient **then**
4:    ATM dispenses cash
5: **else**
6:    ATM displays error
7: **end if**

Remarks:

- A connection problem between the bank and the ATM may block Algorithm 7.1 in Line 2.

- A *network partition* is a failure where a network splits into at least two parts that cannot communicate with each other. Intuitively any non-trivial distributed system cannot proceed during a partition *and* maintain consistency. In the following we introduce the tradeoff between consistency, availability and partition tolerance.

- There are numerous causes for partitions to occur, e.g., physical disconnections, software errors, or incompatible protocol versions. From the point of view of a node in the system, a partition is similar to a period of sustained message loss.

7.1 Consistency, Availability and Partitions

Definition 7.2 (Consistency). *All nodes in the system agree on the current state of the system.*

Definition 7.3 (Availability). *The system is operational and instantly processing incoming requests.*

Definition 7.4 (Partition Tolerance). *Partition tolerance is the ability of a distributed system to continue operating correctly even in the presence of a network partition.*

Theorem 7.5 (CAP Theorem). *It is impossible for a distributed system to simultaneously provide Consistency, Availability and Partition Tolerance. A distributed system can satisfy any two of these but not all three.*

Proof. Assume two nodes, sharing some state. The nodes are in different partitions, i.e., they cannot communicate. Assume a request wants to update the state and contacts a node. The node may either: 1) update its local state, resulting in inconsistent states, or 2) not update its local state, i.e., the system is no longer available for updates. □

Algorithm 7.6 Partition tolerant and available ATM

1: **if** bank reachable **then**
2:    Synchronize local view of balances between ATM and bank
3:    **if** balance of customer insufficient **then**
4:       ATM displays error and aborts user interaction
5:    **end if**
6: **end if**
7: ATM dispenses cash
8: ATM logs withdrawal for synchronization

7.2. BITCOIN

Remarks:

- Algorithm 7.6 is partition tolerant and available since it continues to process requests even when the bank is not reachable.

- The ATM's local view of the balances may diverge from the balances as seen by the bank, therefore consistency is no longer guaranteed.

- The algorithm will synchronize any changes it made to the local balances back to the bank once connectivity is re-established. This is known as eventual consistency.

Definition 7.7 (Eventual Consistency). *If no new updates to the shared state are issued, then eventually the system is in a quiescent state, i.e., no more messages need to be exchanged between nodes, and the shared state is consistent.*

Remarks:

- Eventual consistency is a form of *weak consistency*.

- Eventual consistency guarantees that the state is eventually agreed upon, but the nodes may disagree temporarily.

- During a partition, different updates may semantically conflict with each other. A *conflict resolution* mechanism is required to resolve the conflicts and allow the nodes to eventually agree on a common state.

- One example of eventual consistency is the Bitcoin cryptocurrency system.

7.2 Bitcoin

Definition 7.8 (Bitcoin Network). *The Bitcoin network is a randomly connected overlay network of a few thousand **nodes**, controlled by a variety of owners. All nodes perform the same operations, i.e., it is a homogenous network and without central control.*

Remarks:

- The lack of structure is intentional: it ensures that an attacker cannot strategically position itself in the network and manipulate the information exchange. Information is exchanged via a simple broadcasting protocol.

Definition 7.9 (Address). *Users may generate any number of private keys, from which a public key is then derived. An address is derived from a public key and may be used to identify the recipient of funds in Bitcoin. The private/public key pair is used to uniquely identify the owner of funds of an address.*

Remarks:

- The terms public key and address are often used interchangeably, since both are public information. The advantage of using an address is that its representation is shorter than the public key.

- It is hard to link addresses to the user that controls them, hence Bitcoin is often referred to as being *pseudonymous*.

- Not every user needs to run a fully validating node, and end-users will likely use a lightweight client that only temporarily connects to the network.

- The Bitcoin network collaboratively tracks the balance in bitcoins of each address.

- The address is composed of a network identifier byte, the hash of the public key and a checksum. It is commonly stored in base 58 encoding, a custom encoding similar to base 64 with some ambiguous symbols removed, e.g., lowercase letter "l" since it is similar to the number "1".

- The hashing algorithm produces addresses of size 20 bytes. This means that there are 2^{160} distinct addresses. It might be tempting to brute force a target address, however at one billion trials per second one still requires approximately 2^{45} years in expectation to find a matching private/public key pair. Due to the birthday paradox the odds improve if instead of brute forcing a single address we attempt to brute force any address. While the odds of a successful trial increase with the number of addresses, lookups become more costly.

7.2. BITCOIN

Definition 7.10 (Output). *An output is a tuple consisting of an amount of bitcoins and a spending condition. Most commonly the spending condition requires a valid signature associated with the private key of an address.*

Remarks:

- Spending conditions are scripts that offer a variety of options. Apart from a single signature, they may include conditions that require the result of a simple computation, or the solution to a cryptographic puzzle.

- Outputs exist in two states: unspent and spent. Any output can be spent at most once. The address balance is the sum of bitcoin amounts in unspent outputs that are associated with the address.

- The set of unspent transaction outputs (UTXO) and some additional global parameters is the shared state of Bitcoin. Every node in the Bitcoin network holds a complete replica of that state. Local replicas may temporarily diverge, but consistency is eventually re-established.

Definition 7.11 (Input). *An input is a tuple consisting of a reference to a previously created output and arguments (signature) to the spending condition, proving that the transaction creator has the permission to spend the referenced output.*

Definition 7.12 (Transaction). *A transaction is a datastructure that describes the transfer of bitcoins from spenders to recipients. The transaction consists of a number of inputs and new outputs. The inputs result in the referenced outputs spent (removed from the UTXO), and the new outputs being added to the UTXO.*

Remarks:

- Inputs reference the output that is being spent by a (h, i)-tuple, where h is the hash of the transaction that created the output, and i specifies the index of the output in that transaction.

- Transactions are broadcast in the Bitcoin network and processed by every node that receives them.

Algorithm 7.13 Node Receives Transaction

1: Receive transaction t
2: **for each** input (h, i) in t **do**
3:    **if** output (h, i) is not in local UTXO **or** signature invalid **then**
4:      Drop t and stop
5:    **end if**
6: **end for**
7: **if** sum of values of inputs $<$ sum of values of new outputs **then**
8:    Drop t and stop
9: **end if**
10: **for each** input (h, i) in t **do**
11:    Remove (h, i) from local UTXO
12: **end for**
13: Append t to local history
14: Forward t to neighbors in the Bitcoin network

Remarks:

- Note that the effect of a transaction on the state is deterministic. In other words if all nodes receive the same set of transactions in the same order (Definition 2.8), then the state across nodes is consistent.

- The outputs of a transaction may assign less than the sum of inputs, in which case the difference is called the transaction's *fee*. The fee is used to incentivize other participants in the system (see Definition 7.19)

- Notice that so far we only described a local acceptance policy. Nothing prevents nodes to locally accept different transactions that spend the same output.

- Transactions are in one of two states: unconfirmed or confirmed. Incoming transactions from the broadcast are unconfirmed and added to a pool of transactions called the *memory pool*.

Definition 7.14 (Doublespend). *A doublespend is a situation in which multiple transactions attempt to spend the same output. Only one transaction can be valid since outputs can only be spent once. When nodes accept different transactions in a doublespend, the shared state becomes inconsistent.*

7.2. BITCOIN

Remarks:

- Doublespends may occur naturally, e.g., if outputs are co-owned by multiple users. However, often doublespends are intentional – we call these doublespend-attacks: In a transaction, an attacker pretends to transfer an output to a victim, only to doublespend the same output in another transaction back to itself.

- Doulespends can result in an inconsistent state since the validity of transactions depends on the order in which they arrive. If two conflicting transactions are seen by a node, the node considers the first to be valid, see Algorithm 7.13. The second transaction is invalid since it tries to spend an output that is already spent. The order in which transactions are seen, may not be the same for all nodes, hence the inconsistent state.

- If doublespends are not resolved, the shared state diverges. Therefore a conflict resolution mechanism is needed to decide which of the conflicting transactions is to be confirmed (accepted by everybody), to achieve eventual consistency.

Definition 7.15 (Proof-of-Work). *Proof-of-Work (PoW) is a mechanism that allows a party to prove to another party that a certain amount of computational resources has been utilized for a period of time. A function $\mathcal{F}_d(c, x) \to \{true, false\}$, where difficulty d is a positive number, while challenge c and nonce x are usually bit-strings, is called a Proof-of-Work function if it has following properties:*

1. $\mathcal{F}_d(c, x)$ *is fast to compute if d, c, and x are given.*

2. *For fixed parameters d and c, finding x such that $\mathcal{F}_d(c, x) = true$ is computationally difficult but feasible. The difficulty d is used to adjust the time to find such an x.*

Definition 7.16 (Bitcoin PoW function). *The Bitcoin PoW function is given by*

$$\mathcal{F}_d(c, x) \to \text{SHA256}(\text{SHA256}(c|x)) < \frac{2^{224}}{d}.$$

84 CHAPTER 7. EVENTUAL CONSISTENCY & BITCOIN

Remarks:

- This function concatenates the challenge c and nonce x, and hashes them twice using SHA256. The output of SHA256 is a cryptographic hash with a numeric value in $\{0,\ldots,2^{256}-1\}$ which is compared to a target value $\frac{2^{224}}{d}$, which gets smaller with increasing difficulty.

- SHA256 is a cryptographic hash function with pseudo-random output. No better algorithm is known to find a nonce x such that the function $\mathcal{F}_d(c,x)$ returns true than simply iterating over possible inputs. This is by design to make it difficult to find such an input, but simple to verify the validity once it has been found.

- If the PoW functions of all nodes had the same challenge, the fastest node would always win. However, as we will see in Definition 7.19, each node attempts to find a valid nonce for a node-specific challenge.

Definition 7.17 (Block). *A block is a datastructure used to communicate incremental changes to the local state of a node. A block consists of a list of transactions, a reference to a previous block and a nonce. A block lists some transactions the block creator ("miner") has accepted to its memory-pool since the previous block. A node finds and broadcasts a block when it finds a valid nonce for its PoW function.*

Algorithm 7.18 Node Finds Block

1: Nonce $x = 0$, challenge c, difficulty d, previous block b_{t-1}
2: **repeat**
3:    $x = x + 1$
4: **until** $\mathcal{F}_d(c,x) = true$
5: Broadcast block $b_t = (memory\text{-}pool, b_{t-1}, x)$

Remarks:

- With their reference to a previous block, the blocks build a tree, rooted in the so called *genesis block*.

- The primary goal for using the PoW mechanism is to adjust the rate at which blocks are found in the network, giving the network time to synchronize on the lat-

7.2. BITCOIN

est block. Bitcoin sets the difficulty so that globally a block is created about every 10 minutes in expectation.

- Finding a block allows the finder to impose the transactions in its local memory pool to all other nodes. Upon receiving a block, all nodes roll back any local changes since the previous block and apply the new block's transactions.

- Transactions contained in a block are said to be *confirmed* by that block.

Definition 7.19 (Reward Transaction). *The first transaction in a block is called the reward transaction. The block's miner is rewarded for confirming transactions by allowing it to mint new coins. The reward transaction has a dummy input, and the sum of outputs is determined by a fixed subsidy plus the sum of the fees of transactions confirmed in the block.*

Remarks:

- A reward transaction is the sole exception to the rule that the sum of inputs must be at least the sum of outputs.

- The number of bitcoins that are minted by the reward transaction and assigned to the miner is determined by a subsidy schedule that is part of the protocol. Initially the subsidy was 50 bitcoins for every block, and it is being halved every 210,000 blocks, or 4 years in expectation. Due to the halving of the block reward, the total amount of bitcoins in circulation never exceeds 21 million bitcoins.

- It is expected that the cost of performing the PoW to find a block, in terms of energy and infrastructure, is close to the value of the reward the miner receives from the reward transaction in the block.

Definition 7.20 (Blockchain). *The longest path from the genesis block, i.e., root of the tree, to a leaf is called the blockchain. The blockchain acts as a consistent transaction history on which all nodes eventually agree.*

Remarks:

- The path length from the genesis block to block b is the height h_b.

- Only the longest path from the genesis block to a leaf is a valid transaction history, since branches may contradict each other because of doublespends.

- Since only transactions in the longest path are agreed upon, miners have an incentive to append their blocks to the longest chain, thus agreeing on the current state.

- The mining incentives quickly increased the difficulty of the PoW mechanism: initially miners used CPUs to mine blocks, but CPUs were quickly replaced by GPUs, FPGAs and even application specific integrated circuits (ASICs) as bitcoins appreciated. This results in an equilibrium today in which only the most cost efficient miners, in terms of hardware supply and electricity, make a profit in expectation.

- If multiple blocks are mined more or less concurrently, the system is said to have *forked*. Forks happen naturally because mining is a distributed random process and two new blocks may be found at roughly the same time.

Algorithm 7.21 Node Receives Block

1: Receive block b
2: For this node the current head is block b_{max} at height h_{max}
3: Connect block b in the tree as child of its parent p at height $h_b = h_p + 1$
4: **if** $h_b > h_{max}$ **then**
5:    $h_{max} = h_b$
6:    $b_{max} = b$
7:    Compute UTXO for the path leading to b_{max}
8:    Cleanup memory pool
9: **end if**

7.3. SMART CONTRACTS

Remarks:

- Algorithm 7.21 describes how a node updates its local state upon receiving a block. Notice that, like Algorithm 7.13, this describes the local policy and may also result in node states diverging, i.e., by accepting different blocks at the same height as current head.

- Unlike extending the current path, switching paths may result in confirmed transactions no longer being confirmed, because the blocks in the new path do not include them. Switching paths is referred to as a *reorg*.

- Cleaning up the memory pool involves 1) removing transactions that were confirmed in a block in the current path, 2) removing transactions that conflict with confirmed transactions, and 3) adding transactions that were confirmed in the previous path, but are no longer confirmed in the current path.

- In order to avoid having to recompute the entire UTXO at every new block being added to the blockchain, all current implementations use datastructures that store undo information about the operations applied by a block. This allows efficient switching of paths and updates of the head by moving along the path.

Theorem 7.22. *Forks are eventually resolved and all nodes eventually agree on which is the longest blockchain. The system therefore guarantees eventual consistency.*

Proof. In order for the fork to continue to exist, pairs of blocks need to be found in close succession, extending distinct branches, otherwise the nodes on the shorter branch would switch to the longer one. The probability of branches being extended almost simultaneously decreases exponentially with the length of the fork, hence there will eventually be a time when only one branch is being extended, becoming the longest branch. □

7.3 Smart Contracts

Definition 7.23 (Smart Contract). *A smart contract is an agreement between two or more parties, encoded in such a way that the correct execution is guaranteed by the blockchain.*

Remarks:

- Contracts allow business logic to be encoded in Bitcoin transactions which mutually guarantee that an agreed upon action is performed. The blockchain acts as conflict mediator, should a party fail to honor an agreement.

- The use of scripts as spending conditions for outputs enables smart contracts. Scripts, together with some additional features such as timelocks, allow encoding complex conditions, specifying who may spend the funds associated with an output and when.

Definition 7.24 (Timelock). *Bitcoin provides a mechanism to make transactions invalid until some time in the future: **timelocks**. A transaction may specify a locktime: the earliest time, expressed in either a Unix timestamp or a blockchain height, at which it may be included in a block and therefore be confirmed.*

Remarks:

- Transactions with a timelock are not released into the network until the timelock expires. It is the responsibility of the node receiving the transaction to store it locally until the timelock expires and then release it into the network.

- Transactions with future timelocks are invalid. Blocks may not include transactions with timelocks that have not yet expired, i.e., they are mined before their expiry timestamp or in a lower block than specified. If a block includes an unexpired transaction it is invalid. Upon receiving invalid transactions or blocks, nodes discard them immediately and do not forward them to their peers.

- Timelocks can be used to replace or supersede transactions: a timelocked transaction t_1 can be replaced by another transaction t_0, spending some of the same outputs, if the replacing transaction t_0 has an earlier timelock and can be broadcast in the network before the replaced transaction t_1 becomes valid.

Definition 7.25 (Singlesig and Multisig Outputs). *When an output can be claimed by providing a single signature it is called a **singlesig output**. In contrast the script of **multisig outputs***

7.3. SMART CONTRACTS

specifies a set of m public keys and requires k-of-m (with $k \leq m$) valid signatures from distinct matching public keys from that set in order to be valid.

Remarks:

- Most smart contracts begin with the creation of a 2-of-2 multisig output, requiring a signature from both parties. Once the transaction creating the multisig output is confirmed in the blockchain, both parties are guaranteed that the funds of that output cannot be spent unilaterally.

Algorithm 7.26 Parties A and B create a 2-of-2 multisig output o

1: B sends a list I_B of inputs with c_B coins to A
2: A selects its own inputs I_A with c_A coins
3: A creates transaction $t_s\{[I_A, I_B], [o = c_A + c_B \to (A, B)]\}$
4: A creates timelocked transaction $t_r\{[o], [c_A \to A, c_B \to B]\}$ and signs it
5: A sends t_s and t_r to B
6: B signs both t_s and t_r and sends them to A
7: A signs t_s and broadcasts it to the Bitcoin network

Remarks:

- t_s is called a *setup transaction* and is used to lock in funds into a shared account. If t_s is signed and broadcast immediately, one of the parties could not collaborate to spend the multisig output, and the funds become unspendable. To avoid a situation where the funds cannot be spent, the protocol also creates a timelocked *refund transaction* t_r which guarantees that, should the funds not be spent before the timelock expires, the funds are returned to the respective party. At no point in time one of the parties holds a fully signed setup transaction without the other party holding a fully signed refund transaction, guaranteeing that funds are eventually returned.

- Both transactions require the signature of both parties. In the case of the setup transaction because it has two inputs from A and B respectively which require individual signatures. In the case of the refund transaction the single input spending the multisig output requires both signatures being a 2-of-2 multisig output.

Algorithm 7.27 Simple Micropayment Channel from S to R with capacity c

---
1: $c_S = c$, $c_R = 0$
2: S and R use Algorithm 7.26 to set up output o with value c from S
3: Create settlement transaction $t_f\{[o], [c_S \to S, c_R \to R]\}$
4: **while** channel open **and** $c_R < c$ **do**
5:    In exchange for good with value δ
6:    $c_R = c_R + \delta$
7:    $c_S = c_S - \delta$
8:    Update t_f with outputs $[c_R \to R, c_S \to S]$
9:    S signs and sends t_f to R
10: **end while**
11: R signs last t_f and broadcasts it

Remarks:

- Algorithm 7.27 implements a Simple Micropayment Channel, a smart contract that is used for rapidly adjusting micropayments from a spender to a recipient. Only two transactions are ever broadcast and inserted into the blockchain: the setup transaction t_s and the last settlement transaction t_f. There may have been any number of updates to the settlement transaction, transferring ever more of the shared output to the recipient.

- The number of bitcoins c used to fund the channel is also the maximum total that may be transferred over the simple micropayment channel.

- At any time the recipient R is guaranteed to eventually receive the bitcoins, since she holds a fully signed settlement transaction, while the spender only has partially signed ones.

- The simple micropayment channel is intrinsically unidirectional. Since the recipient may choose any of the settlement transactions in the protocol, she will use the one with maximum payout for her. If we were to transfer bitcoins back, we would be reducing the amount paid out

7.4 Weak Consistency

to the recipient, hence she would choose not to broadcast that transaction.

Eventual consistency is only one form of weak consistency. A number of different tradeoffs between partition tolerance and consistency exist in literature.

Definition 7.28 (Monotonic Read Consistency). *If a node u has seen a particular value of an object, any subsequent accesses of u will never return any older values.*

Remarks:

- Users are annoyed if they receive a notification about a comment on an online social network, but are unable to reply because the web interface does not show the same notification yet. In this case the notification acts as the first read operation, while looking up the comment on the web interface is the second read operation.

Definition 7.29 (Monotonic Write Consistency). *A write operation by a node on a data item is completed before any successive write operation by the same node (i.e. system guarantees to serialize writes by the same node).*

Remarks:

- The ATM must replay all operations in order, otherwise it might happen that an earlier operation overwrites the result of a later operation, resulting in an inconsistent final state.

Definition 7.30 (Read-Your-Write Consistency). *After a node u has updated a data item, any later reads from node u will never see an older value.*

Definition 7.31 (Causal Relation). *The following pairs of operations are said to be causally related:*

- *Two writes by the same node to different variables.*
- *A read followed by a write of the same node.*

- *A read that returns the value of a write from any node.*

- *Two operations that are transitively related according to the above conditions.*

Remarks:

- The first rule ensures that writes by a single node are seen in the same order. For example if a node writes a value in one variable and then signals that it has written the value by writing in another variable. Another node could then read the signalling variable but still read the old value from the first variable, if the two writes were not causally related.

Definition 7.32 (Causal Consistency). *A system provides causal consistency if operations that potentially are causally related are seen by every node of the system in the same order. Concurrent writes are not causally related, and may be seen in different orders by different nodes.*

Chapter Notes

The CAP theorem was first introduced by Fox and Brewer [FB99], although it is commonly attributed to a talk by Eric Brewer [Bre00]. It was later proven by Gilbert and Lynch [GL02] for the asynchronous model. Gilbert and Lynch also showed how to relax the consistency requirement in a partially synchronous system to achieve availability and partition tolerance.

Bitcoin was introduced in 2008 by Satoshi Nakamoto [Nak08]. Nakamoto is thought to be a pseudonym used by either a single person or a group of people; it is still unknown who invented Bitcoin, giving rise to speculation and conspiracy theories. Among the plausible theories are noted cryptographers Nick Szabo [Big13] and Hal Finney [Gre14]. The first Bitcoin client was published shortly after the paper and the first block was mined on January 3, 2009. The genesis block contained the headline of the release date's The Times issue *"The Times 03/Jan/2009 Chancellor on brink of second bailout for banks"*, which serves as proof that the genesis block has been indeed mined on that date, and that no one had mined before that date. The quote in the genesis block is also thought to be an ideological hint: Bitcoin was created in a climate of financial crisis, induced by rampant manipulation by the banking sector, and Bitcoin quickly grew in popularity in anarchic and libertarian circles. The original client is nowadays maintained by a group of independent core developers and remains the most used client in the Bitcoin network.

Central to Bitcoin is the resolution of conflicts due to doublespends, which is solved by waiting for transactions to be included in the blockchain. This however introduces large delays for the confirmation of payments which are undesirable in some scenarios in which an immediate confirmation is required. Karame et al. [KAC12] show that accepting unconfirmed transactions leads to a non-negligible probability of being defrauded as a result of a doublespending attack. This is facilitated by *information eclipsing* [DW13], i.e., that nodes do not forward conflicting transactions, hence the victim does not see both transactions of the doublespend. Bamert et al. [BDE$^+$13] showed that the odds of detecting a doublespending attack in real-time can be improved by connecting to a large sample of nodes and tracing the propagation of transactions in the network.

Bitcoin does not scale very well due to its reliance on confirmations in the blockchain. A copy of the entire transaction history is stored on every node in order to bootstrap joining nodes, which have to reconstruct the transaction history from the genesis block. Simple micropayment channels were introduced by Hearn and Spilman [HS12] and may be used to bundle multiple transfers between two parties but they are limited to transferring the funds locked into the channel once. Recently Duplex Micropayment Channels [DW15] and the Lightning Network [PD15] have been proposed to build bidirectional micropayment channels in which the funds can be transferred back and forth an arbitrary number of times, greatly increasing the flexibility of Bitcoin transfers and enabling a number of features, such as micropayments and routing payments between any two endpoints.

Bibliography

[BDE$^+$13] Tobias Bamert, Christian Decker, Lennart Elsen, Samuel Welten, and Roger Wattenhofer. Have a snack, pay with bitcoin. In *IEEE Internation Conference on Peer-to-Peer Computing (P2P), Trento, Italy*, 2013.

[Big13] John Biggs. Who is the real satoshi nakamoto?

one researcher may have found the answer. http://on.tcrn.ch/l/R0vA, 2013.

[Bre00] Eric A. Brewer. Towards robust distributed systems. In *Symposium on Principles of Distributed Computing (PODC)*. ACM, 2000.

[DW13] Christian Decker and Roger Wattenhofer. Information propagation in the bitcoin network. In *IEEE International Conference on Peer-to-Peer Computing (P2P), Trento, Italy*, September 2013.

[DW15] Christian Decker and Roger Wattenhofer. A Fast and Scalable Payment Network with Bitcoin Duplex Micropayment Channels. In *Symposium on Stabilization, Safety, and Security of Distributed Systems (SSS)*, 2015.

[FB99] Armando Fox and Eric Brewer. Harvest, yield, and scalable tolerant systems. In *Hot Topics in Operating Systems*. IEEE, 1999.

[GL02] Seth Gilbert and Nancy Lynch. Brewer's conjecture and the feasibility of consistent, available, partition-tolerant web services. *SIGACT News*, 2002.

[Gre14] Andy Greenberg. Nakamoto's neighbor: My hunt for bitcoin's creator led to a paralyzed crypto genius. http://onforb.es/1rvyecq, 2014.

[HS12] Mike Hearn and Jeremy Spilman. Contract: Rapidly adjusting micro-payments. https://en.bitcoin.it/wiki/Contract, 2012. Last accessed on November 11, 2015.

[KAC12] G.O. Karame, E. Androulaki, and S. Capkun. Two Bitcoins at the Price of One? Double-Spending Attacks on Fast Payments in Bitcoin. In *Conference on Computer and Communication Security*, 2012.

[Nak08] Satoshi Nakamoto. Bitcoin: A peer-to-peer electronic cash system. https://bitcoin.org/bitcoin.pdf, 2008.

[PD15] Joseph Poon and Thaddeus Dryja. The bitcoin lightning network. 2015.

Chapter 8

Distributed Storage

How do you store 1M movies, each with a size of about 1GB, on 1M nodes, each equipped with a 1TB disk? Simply store the movies on the nodes, arbitrarily, and memorize (with a global index) which movie is stored on which node. What if the set of movies or nodes changes over time, and you do not want to change your global index too often?

8.1 Consistent Hashing

Several variants of hashing will do the job, e.g. consistent hashing:

Algorithm 8.1 Consistent Hashing

1: Hash the unique file name of each movie m with a known set of hash functions $h_i(m) \to [0, 1)$, for $i = 1, \ldots, k$
2: Hash the unique name (e.g., IP address and port number) of each node with the same set of hash functions h_i, for $i = 1, \ldots, k$
3: Store a copy of a movie x on node u if $h_i(x) \approx h_i(u)$, for any i. More formally, store movie x on node u if

$$|h_i(x) - h_i(u)| = \min_m \{|h_i(m) - h_i(u)|\}, \text{ for any } i$$

Theorem 8.2 (Consistent Hashing). *In expectation, Algorithm 8.1 stores each movie kn/m times.*

Proof. While it is possible that some movie does not hash closest to a node for any of its hash functions, this is highly unlikely: For each node (n) and each hash function (k), each movie has about the same probability ($1/m$) to be stored. By linearity of expectation, a movie is stored kn/m times, in expectation. □

Remarks:

- Let us do a back-of-the-envelope calculation. We have $m = 1M$ movies, $n = 1M$ nodes, each node has storage for $1TB/1GB = 1K$ movies, i.e., we use $k = 1K$ hash functions. Theorem 8.2 shows that each movie is stored about 1K times. With a bit more math one can show that it is highly unlikely that a movie is stored much less often than its expected value.

- Instead of storing movies directly on nodes as in Algorithm 8.1, we can also store the movies on any nodes we like. The nodes of Algorithm 8.1 then simply store forward pointers to the actual movie locations.

- In this chapter we want to push unreliability to the extreme. What if the nodes are so unreliable that on average a node is only available for 1 hour? In other words, nodes exhibit a high *churn*, they constantly join and leave the distributed system.

- With such a high churn, hundreds or thousands of nodes will change every second. No single node can have an accurate picture of what other nodes are currently in the system. This is remarkably different to classic distributed systems, where a single unavailable node may already be a minor disaster: all the other nodes have to get a consistent view (Definition 5.4) of the system again. In high churn systems it is impossible to have a consistent view at any time.

- Instead, each node will just know about a small subset of 100 or less other nodes ("neighbors"). This way, nodes can withstand high churn situations.

- On the downside, nodes will not directly know which node is responsible for what movie. Instead, a node searching for a movie might have to ask a neighbor node, which in turn will recursively ask another neighbor node, until the correct node storing the movie (or a forward pointer to the movie) is found. The nodes of our distributed storage system form a virtual network, also called an *overlay network*.

8.2 Hypercubic Networks

In this section we present a few overlay topologies of general interest.

Definition 8.3 (Topology Properties). *Our virtual network should have the following properties:*

- *The network should be (somewhat) **homogeneous**: no node should play a dominant role, no node should be a single point of failure.*

- *The nodes should have **IDs**, and the IDs should span the universe $[0, 1)$, such that we can store data with hashing, as in Algorithm 8.1.*

- *Every node should have a small **degree**, if possible polylogarithmic in n, the number of nodes. This will allow every node to maintain a persistent connection with each neighbor, which will help us to deal with churn.*

- *The network should have a small **diameter**, and routing should be easy. If a node does not have the information about a data item, then it should know which neighbor to ask. Within a few (polylogarithmic in n) hops, one should find the node that has the correct information.*

Remarks:

- Some basic network topologies used in practice are trees, rings, grids or tori. Many other suggested networks are simply combinations or derivatives of these.

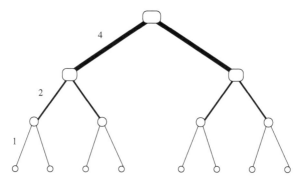

Figure 8.4: The structure of a fat tree.

- The advantage of trees is that the routing is very easy: for every source-destination pair there is only one path. However, since the root of a tree is a bottleneck, trees are not homogeneous. Instead, so-called *fat trees* should be used. Fat trees have the property that every edge connecting a node v to its parent u has a capacity that is proportional to the number of leaves of the subtree rooted at v. See Figure 8.4 for a picture.

- Fat trees belong to a family of networks that require edges of non-uniform capacity to be efficient. Networks with edges of uniform capacity are easier to build. This is usually the case for grids and tori. Unless explicitly mentioned, we will treat all edges in the following to be of capacity 1.

Definition 8.5 (Torus, Mesh)**.** *Let $m, d \in \mathbb{N}$. The (m, d)-mesh $M(m, d)$ is a graph with node set $V = [m]^d$ and edge set*

$$E = \left\{ \{(a_1, \ldots, a_d), (b_1, \ldots, b_d)\} \mid a_i, b_i \in [m], \sum_{i=1}^{d} |a_i - b_i| = 1 \right\},$$

where $[m]$ means the set $\{0, \ldots, m-1\}$. The (m, d)-torus $T(m, d)$ is a graph that consists of an (m, d)-mesh and additionally wrap-around edges from nodes $(a_1, \ldots, a_{i-1}, m-1, a_{i+1}, \ldots, a_d)$ to nodes $(a_1, \ldots, a_{i-1}, 0, a_{i+1}, \ldots, a_d)$ for all $i \in \{1, \ldots, d\}$ and all $a_j \in [m]$ with $j \neq i$. In other words, we take the expression $a_i - b_i$ in the sum modulo m prior to computing the absolute value. $M(m, 1)$ is

8.2. HYPERCUBIC NETWORKS

also called a **path**, $T(m,1)$ a **cycle**, and $M(2,d) = T(2,d)$ a **d-dimensional hypercube**. Figure 8.6 presents a linear array, a torus, and a hypercube.

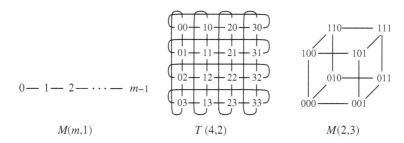

Figure 8.6: The structure of $M(m,1)$, $T(4,2)$, and $M(2,3)$.

Remarks:

- Routing on a mesh, torus, or hypercube is trivial. On a d-dimensional hypercube, to get from a source bitstring s to a target bitstring t one only needs to fix each "wrong" bit, one at a time; in other words, if the source and the target differ by k bits, there are $k!$ routes with k hops.

- If you put a dot in front of the d-bit ID of each node, the nodes exactly span the d-bit IDs $[0,1)$.

- The Chord architecture is a close relative of the hypercube, basically a less rigid hypercube. The hypercube connects every node with an ID in $[0,1)$ with every node in *exactly* distance 2^{-i}, $i = 1, 2, \ldots, d$ in $[0,1)$. Chord instead connect nodes with *approximately* distance 2^{-i}.

- The hypercube has many derivatives, the so-called *hypercubic networks*. Among these are the butterfly, cube-connected-cycles, shuffle-exchange, and de Bruijn graph. We start with the butterfly, which is basically a "rolled out" hypercube.

Definition 8.7 (Butterfly). *Let $d \in \mathbb{N}$. The d-dimensional butterfly $BF(d)$ is a graph with node set $V = [d+1] \times [2]^d$ and an edge set $E = E_1 \cup E_2$ with*

$$E_1 = \{\{(i,\alpha),(i+1,\alpha)\} \mid i \in [d], \alpha \in [2^d]\}$$

and

$$E_2 = \{\{(i,\alpha),(i+1,\beta)\} \mid i \in [d],\ \alpha,\beta \in [2^d], |\alpha-\beta| = 2^i\}.$$

A node set $\{(i,\alpha) \mid \alpha \in [2]^d\}$ *is said to form* **level** i *of the butterfly. The d-**dimensional wrap-around butterfly** W-BF(d) is defined by taking the BF(d) and having* $(d,\alpha) = (0,\alpha)$ *for all* $\alpha \in [2]^d$.

Remarks:

- Figure 8.8 shows the 3-dimensional butterfly $BF(3)$. The $BF(d)$ has $(d+1)2^d$ nodes, $2d \cdot 2^d$ edges and degree 4. It is not difficult to check that combining the node sets $\{(i,\alpha) \mid i \in [d]\}$ for all $\alpha \in [2]^d$ into a single node results in the hypercube.

- Butterflies have the advantage of a constant node degree over hypercubes, whereas hypercubes feature more fault-tolerant routing.

- You may have seen butterfly-like structures before, e.g. sorting networks, communication switches, data center networks, fast fourier transform (FFT). The Benes network (telecommunication) is nothing but two back-to-back butterflies. The Clos network (data centers) is a close relative to Butterflies too. Actually, merging the 2^i nodes on level i that share the first $d-i$ bits into a single node, the Butterfly becomes a fat tree. Every year there are new applications for which hypercubic networks are the perfect solution!

- Next we define the cube-connected-cycles network. It only has a degree of 3 and it results from the hypercube by replacing the corners by cycles.

Definition 8.9 (Cube-Connected-Cycles)**.** *Let* $d \in \mathbb{N}$. *The* **cube-connected-cycles** *network* $CCC(d)$ *is a graph with node set* $V = \{(a,p) \mid a \in [2]^d, p \in [d]\}$ *and edge set*

$$\begin{aligned}E = & \{\{(a,p),(a,(p+1) \bmod d)\} \mid a \in [2]^d, p \in [d]\} \\ & \cup \{\{(a,p),(b,p)\} \mid a,b \in [2]^d, p \in [d], a = b \text{ except for } a_p\}\ .\end{aligned}$$

8.2. HYPERCUBIC NETWORKS

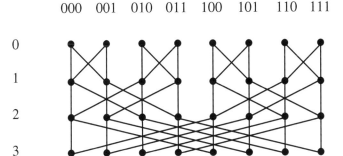

Figure 8.8: The structure of BF(3).

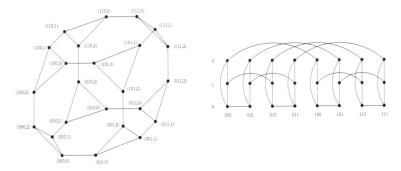

Figure 8.10: The structure of CCC(3).

Remarks:

- Two possible representations of a CCC can be found in Figure 8.10.

- The shuffle-exchange is yet another way of transforming the hypercubic interconnection structure into a constant degree network.

Definition 8.11 (Shuffle-Exchange). *Let $d \in \mathbb{N}$. The d-dimensional shuffle-exchange $SE(d)$ is defined as an undirected graph with node set $V = [2]^d$ and an edge set $E = E_1 \cup E_2$ with*

$$E_1 = \{\{(a_1,\ldots,a_d),(a_1,\ldots,\bar{a}_d)\} \mid (a_1,\ldots,a_d) \in [2]^d,\ \bar{a}_d = 1-a_d\}$$

and

$$E_2 = \{\{(a_1,\ldots,a_d),(a_d,a_1,\ldots,a_{d-1})\} \mid (a_1,\ldots,a_d) \in [2]^d\} \ .$$

Figure 8.12 shows the 3- and 4-dimensional shuffle-exchange graph.

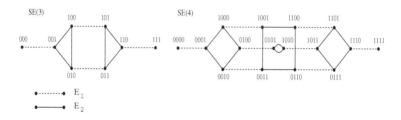

Figure 8.12: The structure of SE(3) and SE(4).

Definition 8.13 (DeBruijn)**.** *The b-**ary DeBruijn graph of dimension** d $DB(b,d)$ is an undirected graph $G = (V, E)$ with node set $V = \{v \in [b]^d\}$ and edge set E that contains all edges $\{v, w\}$ with the property that $w \in \{(x, v_1, \ldots, v_{d-1}) : x \in [b]\}$, where $v = (v_1, \ldots, v_d)$.*

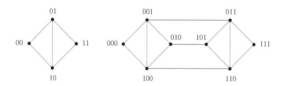

Figure 8.14: The structure of $DB(2,2)$ and $DB(2,3)$.

Remarks:

- Two examples of a DeBruijn graph can be found in Figure 8.14.

- There are some data structures which also qualify as hypercubic networks. An example of a hypercubic network is the skip list, the balanced binary search tree for the lazy programmer:

8.2. HYPERCUBIC NETWORKS

Definition 8.15 (Skip List). *The skip list is an ordinary ordered linked list of objects, augmented with additional forward links. The ordinary linked list is the level 0 of the skip list. In addition, every object is promoted to level 1 with probability 1/2. As for level 0, all level 1 objects are connected by a linked list. In general, every object on level i is promoted to the next level with probability $1/2$. A special start-object points to the smallest/first object on each level.*

Remarks:

- Search, insert, and delete can be implemented in $\mathcal{O}(\log n)$ expected time in a skip list, simply by jumping from higher levels to lower ones when overshooting the searched position. Also, the amortized memory cost of each object is constant, as on average an object only has two forward links.

- The randomization can easily be discarded, by deterministically promoting a constant fraction of objects of level i to level $i + 1$, for all i. When inserting or deleting, object o simply checks whether its left and right level i neighbors are being promoted to level $i + 1$. If none of them is, promote object o itself. Essentially we establish a maximal independent set (MIS) on each level, hence at least every third and at most every second object is promoted.

- There are obvious variants of the skip list, e.g., the skip graph. Instead of promoting only half of the nodes to the next level, we always promote all the nodes, similarly to a balanced binary tree: All nodes are part of the root level of the binary tree. Half the nodes are promoted left, and half the nodes are promoted right, on each level. Hence on level i we have have 2^i lists (or, if we connect the last element again with the first: rings) of about $n/2^i$ objects. The skip graph features all the properties of Definition 8.3.

- More generally, how are degree and diameter of Definition 8.3 related? The following theorem gives a general lower bound.

Theorem 8.16. *Every graph of maximum degree $d > 2$ and size n must have a diameter of at least $\lceil (\log n)/(\log(d-1)) \rceil - 2$.*

Proof. Suppose we have a graph $G = (V, E)$ of maximum degree d and size n. Start from any node $v \in V$. In a first step at most d other nodes can be reached. In two steps at most $d \cdot (d-1)$ additional nodes can be reached. Thus, in general, in at most k steps at most

$$1 + \sum_{i=0}^{k-1} d \cdot (d-1)^i = 1 + d \cdot \frac{(d-1)^k - 1}{(d-1) - 1} \leq \frac{d \cdot (d-1)^k}{d-2}$$

nodes (including v) can be reached. This has to be at least n to ensure that v can reach all other nodes in V within k steps. Hence,

$$(d-1)^k \geq \frac{(d-2) \cdot n}{d} \quad \Leftrightarrow \quad k \geq \log_{d-1}((d-2) \cdot n/d) \ .$$

Since $\log_{d-1}((d-2)/d) > -2$ for all $d > 2$, this is true only if $k \geq \lceil (\log n)/(\log(d-1)) \rceil - 2$. □

Remarks:

- In other words, constant-degree hypercubic networks feature an asymptotically optimal diameter.

- Other hypercubic graphs manage to have a different tradeoff between node degree and diameter. The pancake graph, for instance, minimizes the maximum of these with $d = k = \Theta(\log n / \log \log n)$. The ID of a node u in the pancake graph of dimension d is an arbitrary permutation of the numbers $1, 2, \ldots, d$. Two nodes u, v are connected by an edge if one can get the ID of node v by taking the ID of node u, and reversing (flipping) the first i numbers of u's ID. For example, in dimension $d = 4$, nodes $u = 2314$ and $v = 1324$ are neighbors.

- There are a few other interesting graph classes which are not hypercubic networks, but nevertheless seem to relate to the properties of Definition 8.3. Small-world graphs (a popular representations for social networks) also have small diameter, however, in contrast to hypercubic networks, they are not homogeneous and feature nodes with large degrees.

- Expander graphs (an expander graph is a sparse graph which has good connectivity properties, that is, from every not too large subset of nodes you are connected to an even larger set of nodes) are homogeneous, have a low degree and small diameter. However, expanders are often not routable.

8.3 DHT & Churn

Definition 8.17 (Distributed Hash Table (DHT)). *A **distributed hash table** (DHT) is a distributed data structure that implements a distributed storage. A DHT should support at least (i) a search (for a key) and (ii) an insert (key, object) operation, possibly also (iii) a delete (key) operation.*

Remarks:

- A DHT has many applications beyond storing movies, e.g., the Internet domain name system (DNS) is essentially a DHT.

- A DHT can be implemented as a hypercubic overlay network with nodes having identifiers such that they span the ID space $[0, 1)$.

- A hypercube can directly be used for a DHT. Just use a globally known set of hash functions h_i, mapping movies to bit strings with d bits.

- Other hypercubic structures may be a bit more intricate when using it as a DHT: The butterfly network, for instance, may directly use the $d+1$ layers for replication, i.e., all the $d+1$ nodes are responsible for the same ID.

- Other hypercubic networks, e.g. the pancake graph, might need a bit of twisting to find appropriate IDs.

- We assume that a joining node knows a node which already belongs to the system. This is known as the bootstrap problem. Typical solutions are: If a node has been connected with the DHT previously, just try some of these previous nodes. Or the node may ask some authority for a list of IP addresses (and ports) of nodes that are regularly part of the DHT.

- Many DHTs in the literature are analyzed against an adversary that can crash a fraction of random nodes. After crashing a few nodes the system is given sufficient time to recover again. However, this seems unrealistic. The scheme sketched in this section significantly differs from this in two major aspects.

- First, we assume that joins and leaves occur in a worst-case manner. We think of an adversary that can remove and add a bounded number of nodes; the adversary can choose which nodes to crash and how nodes join.

- Second, the adversary does not have to wait until the system is recovered before it crashes the next batch of nodes. Instead, the adversary can constantly crash nodes, while the system is trying to stay alive. Indeed, the system is *never fully repaired* but *always fully functional*. In particular, the system is resilient against an adversary that continuously attacks the "weakest part" of the system. The adversary could for example insert a crawler into the DHT, learn the topology of the system, and then repeatedly crash selected nodes, in an attempt to partition the DHT. The system counters such an adversary by continuously moving the remaining or newly joining nodes towards the areas under attack.

- Clearly, we cannot allow the adversary to have unbounded capabilities. In particular, in any constant time interval, the adversary can at most add and/or remove $O(\log n)$ nodes, n being the total number of nodes currently in the system. This model covers an adversary which repeatedly takes down nodes by a distributed denial of service attack, however only a logarithmic number of nodes at each point in time. The algorithm relies on messages being delivered timely, in at most constant time between any pair of operational nodes, i.e., the synchronous model. Using the trivial synchronizer this is not a problem. We only need bounded message delays in order to have a notion of time which is needed for the adversarial model. The duration of a round is then proportional to the propagation delay of the slowest message.

8.3. DHT & CHURN

Algorithm 8.18 DHT

1: Given: a globally known set of hash functions h_i, and a hypercube (or any other hypercubic network)
2: Each hypercube virtual node ("hypernode") consists of $\Theta(\log n)$ nodes.
3: Nodes have connections to all other nodes of their hypernode and to nodes of their neighboring hypernodes.
4: Because of churn, some of the nodes have to change to another hypernode such that up to constant factors, all hypernodes own the same number of nodes at all times.
5: If the total number of nodes n grows or shrinks above or below a certain threshold, the dimension of the hypercube is increased or decreased by one, respectively.

Remarks:

- Having a logarithmic number of hypercube neighbors, each with a logarithmic number of nodes, means that each node has $\Theta(\log^2 n)$ neighbors. However, with some additional bells and whistles one can achieve $\Theta(\log n)$ neighbor nodes.

- The balancing of nodes among the hypernodes can be seen as a dynamic token distribution problem on the hypercube. Each hypernode has a certain number of tokens, the goal is to distribute the tokens along the edges of the graph such that all hypernodes end up with the same or almost the same number of tokens. While tokens are moved around, an adversary constantly inserts and deletes tokens. See also Figure 8.19.

- In summary, the storage system builds on two basic components: (i) an algorithm which performs the described dynamic token distribution and (ii) an information aggregation algorithm which is used to estimate the number of nodes in the system and to adapt the dimension of the hypercube accordingly:

Theorem 8.20 (DHT with Churn). *We have a fully scalable, efficient distributed storage system which tolerates $O(\log n)$ worst-case joins and/or crashes per constant time interval. As in other storage systems, nodes have $O(\log n)$ overlay neighbors, and the usual operations (e.g., search, insert) take time $O(\log n)$.*

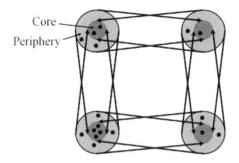

Figure 8.19: A simulated 2-dimensional hypercube with four hypernodes, each consisting of several nodes. Also, all the nodes are either in the core or in the periphery of a node. All nodes within the same hypernode are completely connected to each other, and additionally, all nodes of a hypernode are connected to the core nodes of the neighboring nodes. Only the core nodes store data items, while the peripheral nodes move between the nodes to balance biased adversarial churn.

Remarks:

- Indeed, handling churn is only a minimal requirement to make a distributed storage system work. Advanced studies proposed more elaborate architectures which can also handle other security issues, e.g., privacy or Byzantine attacks.

Chapter Notes

The ideas behind distributed storage were laid during the peer-to-peer (P2P) file sharing hype around the year 2000, so a lot of the seminal research in this area is labeled P2P. The paper of Plaxton, Rajaraman, and Richa [PRR97] laid out a blueprint for many so-called structured P2P architecture proposals, such as Chord [SMK+01], CAN [RFH+01], Pastry [RD01], Viceroy [MNR02], Kademlia [MM02], Koorde [KK03], SkipGraph [AS03], SkipNet [HJS+03], or Tapestry [ZHS+04]. Also the paper of Plaxton et. al. was standing on the shoulders of giants. Some of its eminent precursors are: linear and consistent hashing [KLL+97], locating shared objects [AP90, AP91], compact routing [SK85, PU88], and even earlier: hypercubic networks, e.g. [AJ75, Wit81, GS81, BA84].

Furthermore, the techniques in use for prefix-based overlay structures are related to a proposal called LAND, a locality-aware distributed hash table proposed by Abraham et al. [AMD04].

More recently, a lot of P2P research focussed on security aspects, describing for instance attacks [LMSW06, SENB07, Lar07], and provable countermeasures [KSW05, AS09, BSS09]. Another topic currently garnering interest is using P2P to help distribute live streams of video content on a large scale [LMSW07]. There are several recommendable introductory books on P2P computing, e.g. [SW05, SG05, MS07, KW08, BYL08].

Bibliography

[AJ75] George A. Anderson and E. Douglas Jensen. Computer Interconnection Structures: Taxonomy, Characteristics, and Examples. *ACM Comput. Surv.*, 7(4):197–213, December 1975.

[AMD04] Ittai Abraham, Dahlia Malkhi, and Oren Dobzinski. LAND: stretch (1 + epsilon) locality-aware networks for DHTs. In *Proceedings of the fifteenth annual ACM-SIAM symposium on Discrete algorithms*, SODA '04, pages 550–559, Philadelphia, PA, USA, 2004. Society for Industrial and Applied Mathematics.

[AP90] Baruch Awerbuch and David Peleg. Efficient Distributed Construction of Sparse Covers. Technical report, The Weizmann Institute of Science, 1990.

[AP91] Baruch Awerbuch and David Peleg. Concurrent Online Tracking of Mobile Users. In *SIGCOMM*, pages 221–233, 1991.

[AS03] James Aspnes and Gauri Shah. Skip Graphs. In *SODA*, pages 384–393. ACM/SIAM, 2003.

[AS09] Baruch Awerbuch and Christian Scheideler. Towards a Scalable and Robust DHT. *Theory Comput. Syst.*, 45(2):234–260, 2009.

[BA84] L. N. Bhuyan and D. P. Agrawal. Generalized Hypercube and Hyperbus Structures for a Computer Network. *IEEE Trans. Comput.*, 33(4):323–333, April 1984.

[BSS09] Matthias Baumgart, Christian Scheideler, and Stefan Schmid. A DoS-resilient information system for dynamic data management. In *Proceedings of the twenty-first annual symposium on Parallelism in algorithms and architectures*, SPAA '09, pages 300–309, New York, NY, USA, 2009. ACM.

[BYL08] John Buford, Heather Yu, and Eng Keong Lua. *P2P Networking and Applications*. Morgan Kaufmann Publishers Inc., San Francisco, CA, USA, 2008.

[GS81] J.R. Goodman and C.H. Sequin. Hypertree: A Multiprocessor Interconnection Topology. *Computers, IEEE Transactions on*, C-30(12):923–933, dec. 1981.

[HJS+03] Nicholas J. A. Harvey, Michael B. Jones, Stefan Saroiu, Marvin Theimer, and Alec Wolman. SkipNet: a scalable overlay network with practical locality properties. In *Proceedings of the 4th conference on USENIX Symposium on Internet Technologies and Systems - Volume 4*, USITS'03, pages 9–9, Berkeley, CA, USA, 2003. USENIX Association.

[KK03] M. Frans Kaashoek and David R. Karger. Koorde: A Simple Degree-Optimal Distributed Hash Table. In M. Frans Kaashoek and Ion Stoica, editors, *IPTPS*, volume 2735 of *Lecture Notes in Computer Science*, pages 98–107. Springer, 2003.

[KLL+97] David R. Karger, Eric Lehman, Frank Thomson Leighton, Rina Panigrahy, Matthew S. Levine, and Daniel Lewin. Consistent Hashing and Random Trees: Distributed Caching Protocols for Relieving Hot Spots on the World Wide Web. In Frank Thomson Leighton and Peter W. Shor, editors, *STOC*, pages 654–663. ACM, 1997.

[KSW05] Fabian Kuhn, Stefan Schmid, and Roger Wattenhofer. A Self-Repairing Peer-to-Peer System Resilient to Dynamic Adversarial Churn. In *4th International Workshop on Peer-To-Peer Systems (IPTPS), Cornell University, Ithaca, New York, USA, Springer LNCS 3640*, February 2005.

[KW08] Javed I. Khan and Adam Wierzbicki. Introduction: Guest editors' introduction: Foundation of peer-to-peer computing. *Comput. Commun.*, 31(2):187–189, February 2008.

[Lar07] Erik Larkin. Storm Worm's virulence may change tactics. http://www.networkworld.com/news/2007/080207-black-hat-storm-worms-virulence.html, Agust 2007. Last accessed on June 11, 2012.

[LMSW06] Thomas Locher, Patrick Moor, Stefan Schmid, and Roger Wattenhofer. Free Riding in BitTorrent is Cheap. In *5th Workshop on Hot Topics in Networks (HotNets), Irvine, California, USA*, November 2006.

[LMSW07] Thomas Locher, Remo Meier, Stefan Schmid, and Roger Wattenhofer. Push-to-Pull Peer-to-Peer Live Streaming. In *21st International Symposium on Distributed Computing (DISC), Lemesos, Cyprus*, September 2007.

[MM02] Petar Maymounkov and David Mazières. Kademlia: A Peer-to-Peer Information System Based on the XOR Metric. In *Revised Papers from the First International Workshop on Peer-to-Peer Systems*, IPTPS '01, pages 53–65, London, UK, UK, 2002. Springer-Verlag.

[MNR02] Dahlia Malkhi, Moni Naor, and David Ratajczak. Viceroy: a scalable and dynamic emulation of the butterfly. In *Proceedings of the twenty-first annual symposium on Principles of distributed computing*, PODC '02, pages 183–192, New York, NY, USA, 2002. ACM.

[MS07] Peter Mahlmann and Christian Schindelhauer. *Peer-to-Peer Networks*. Springer, 2007.

[PRR97] C. Greg Plaxton, Rajmohan Rajaraman, and Andréa W. Richa. Accessing Nearby Copies of Replicated Objects in a Distributed Environment. In *SPAA*, pages 311–320, 1997.

[PU88] David Peleg and Eli Upfal. A tradeoff between space and efficiency for routing tables. In *Proceedings of the twentieth annual ACM symposium on Theory of computing*, STOC '88, pages 43–52, New York, NY, USA, 1988. ACM.

[RD01] Antony Rowstron and Peter Druschel. Pastry: Scalable, decentralized object location and routing for large-scale peer-to-peer systems. In *IFIP/ACM International Conference on Distributed Systems Platforms (Middleware)*, pages 329–350, November 2001.

[RFH+01] Sylvia Ratnasamy, Paul Francis, Mark Handley, Richard Karp, and Scott Shenker. A scalable content-addressable network. *SIGCOMM Comput. Commun. Rev.*, 31(4):161–172, August 2001.

[SENB07] Moritz Steiner, Taoufik En-Najjary, and Ernst W. Biersack. Exploiting KAD: possible uses and misuses. *SIGCOMM Comput. Commun. Rev.*, 37(5):65–70, October 2007.

[SG05] Ramesh Subramanian and Brian D. Goodman. *Peer to Peer Computing: The Evolution of a Disruptive Technology*. IGI Publishing, Hershey, PA, USA, 2005.

[SK85] Nicola Santoro and Ramez Khatib. Labelling and Implicit Routing in Networks. *Comput. J.*, 28(1):5–8, 1985.

[SMK+01] Ion Stoica, Robert Morris, David Karger, M. Frans Kaashoek, and Hari Balakrishnan. Chord: A scalable peer-to-peer lookup service for internet applications. *SIGCOMM Comput. Commun. Rev.*, 31(4):149–160, August 2001.

[SW05] Ralf Steinmetz and Klaus Wehrle, editors. *Peer-to-Peer Systems and Applications*, volume 3485 of *Lecture Notes in Computer Science*. Springer, 2005.

[Wit81] L. D. Wittie. Communication Structures for Large Networks of Microcomputers. *IEEE Trans. Comput.*, 30(4):264–273, April 1981.

[ZHS+04] Ben Y. Zhao, Ling Huang, Jeremy Stribling, Sean C. Rhea, Anthony D. Joseph, and John Kubiatowicz. Tapestry: a resilient global-scale overlay for service deployment. *IEEE Journal on Selected Areas in Communications*, 22(1):41–53, 2004.

Index

access strategy, 62
agreement, 18
all-same validity, 34
any-input validity, 34
asynchronous byzantine agreement, 41
asynchronous distributed system, 18
asynchronous runtime, 19
authenticated byzantine agreement, 46
authentication, 45
availability, 78

B-grid quorum system, 68
bitcoin address, 80
bitcoin block, 84
bitcoin network, 79
bivalent configuration, 20
block algorithm, 86
blockchain, 7, 85
butterfly topology, 99
byzantine agreement, 33
byzantine agreement with one fault, 35
byzantine behavior, 33

CAP, 78
causal consistency, 92
causal relation, 91
churn, 107
client server algorithm, 6
client server with acknowledgments, 6

command, 48
commit certificate, 50
complete command, 48
concurrent locking strategy, 66
configuration of a system, 19
configuration transition, 21
configuration tree, 21
consensus, 18
consistency, 78
consistent hashing, 95
correct-input validity, 34
critical configuration, 22
cube-connected-cycles topology, 100

DeBruijn topology, 102
DHT, 105
DHT algorithm, 107
distributed hash table, 105
doublespend, 82

eventual consistency, 79

f-disseminating quorum system, 70
f-masking grid quorum system, 71
f-masking quorum system, 70
f-opaque quorum system, 72
failure probability, 67

grid quorum system, 64

history of commands, 48

INDEX

homogeneous system, 97
hypercube topology, 98
hypercubic network, 97

king algorithm, 38

live system, 57
liveness, 57
load of a quorum system, 62

M-grid quorum system, 72
majority quorum system, 62
median validity, 35
mesh topology, 98
message loss model, 6
message passing model, 5
micropayment channel, 90
mining algorithm, 84
monotonic read consistency, 91
monotonic write consistency, 91
multisig output, 88

node, 5

operation, 48

partition tolerance, 78
paxos algorithm, 13
proof of misbehavior, 50
proof of work, 83
pseudonymous, 80

quorum, 61
quorum system, 61

randomized consensus algorithm, 25
read-your-write consistency, 91
refund transaction, 89
request, 48
resilience of a quorum system, 66
reward transaction, 85

safe system, 51
safety, 51
sequential locking strategy, 65
serializer, 8
setup transaction, 89
SHA256, 84
shared coin algorithm, 29
shuffle-exchange network, 101
signature, 45
singlesig output, 88
singleton quorum system, 62
skip list topology, 103
smart contract, 87
state replication, 7
state replication with serializer, 8
synchronous distributed system, 35
synchronous runtime, 35

termination, 18
ticket, 10
timelock, 88
torus topology, 98
transaction, 81
transaction algorithm, 82
transaction input, 81
transaction output, 81
two-phase commit, 9
two-phase locking, 9
two-phase protocol, 8

univalent configuration, 19

validity, 18
variable message delay model, 7
view change, 53
view of a distributed system, 47

weak consistency, 91
work of a quorum system, 62

zyzzyva algorithm, 48

Printed in Poland
by Amazon Fulfillment
Poland Sp. z o.o., Wrocław